MW01284363

The Essence
of Software
Engineering

FREE
Online Edition

Safari Books Online

Your purchase of *The Essence of Software Engineering: Applying the SEMAT Kernel* includes access to a free online edition for 45 days through the **Safari Books Online** subscription service. Nearly every Addison-Wesley Professional book is available online through **Safari Books Online**, along with thousands of books and videos from publishers such as Cisco Press, Exam Cram, IBM Press, O'Reilly Media, Prentice Hall, Que, Sams, and VMware Press.

Safari Books Online is a digital library providing searchable, on-demand access to thousands of technology, digital media, and professional development books and videos from leading publishers. With one monthly or yearly subscription price, you get unlimited access to learning tools and information on topics including mobile app and software development, tips and tricks on using your favorite gadgets, networking, project management, graphic design, and much more.

Activate your FREE Online Edition at
informit.com/safarifree

STEP 1:   Enter the coupon code: PLCUFWH.

STEP 2:   New Safari users, complete the brief registration form.
Safari subscribers, just log in.

If you have difficulty registering on Safari or accessing the online edition,
please e-mail customer-service@safaribooksonline.com

Try Safari Books Online FREE for 15 days

Get online access to Thousands of Books and Videos

Safari Books Online

FREE 15-DAY TRIAL + 15% OFF*
informit.com/safaritrial

Feed your brain
Gain unlimited access to thousands of books and videos about technology,
digital media and professional development from O'Reilly Media,
Addison-Wesley, Microsoft Press, Cisco Press, McGraw Hill, Wiley, WROX,
Prentice Hall, Que, Sams, Apress, Adobe Press and other top publishers.

See it, believe it
Watch hundreds of expert-led instructional videos on today's hottest topics.

WAIT, THERE'S MORE!

Gain a competitive edge
Be first to learn about the newest technologies and subjects with Rough Cuts
pre-published manuscripts and new technology overviews in Short Cuts.

Accelerate your project
Copy and paste code, create smart searches that let you know when new
books about your favorite topics are available, and customize your library
with favorites, highlights, tags, notes, mash-ups and more.

* Available to new subscribers only. Discount applies to the Safari Library and is valid for first
12 consecutive monthly billing cycles. Safari Library is not available in all countries.

 Addison Wesley Adobe Press Cisco Press   Press   IBM Press   Microsoft Press   New Riders O'REILLY

 Peachpit Press PEARSON IT Certification   PRENTICE HALL   QUE   SAMS   vmware PRESS   WILEY   wrox

 **inform IT.com** THE TRUSTED TECHNOLOGY LEARNING SOURCE

 PEARSON

InformIT is a brand of Pearson and the online presence
for the world's leading technology publishers. It's your source
for reliable and qualified content and knowledge, providing access
to the top brands, authors, and contributors from
the tech community.

↝Addison-Wesley **Cisco Press** EXAM/**CRAM** **IBM** Press. QUE PRENTICE HALL S**A**MS | Safari Books Online

LearnIT at InformIT

Looking for a book, eBook, or training video on a new technology? Seeking
timely and relevant information and tutorials? Looking for expert opinions,
advice, and tips? **InformIT has the solution.**

- Learn about new releases and special promotions by
  subscribing to a wide variety of newsletters.
  Visit **informit.com/newsletters**.

- Access FREE podcasts from experts at **informit.com/podcasts**.

- Read the latest author articles and sample chapters at
  informit.com/articles.

- Access thousands of books and videos in the Safari Books
  Online digital library at **safari.informit.com**.

- Get tips from expert blogs at **informit.com/blogs**.

Visit **informit.com/learn** to discover all the ways you can access the hottest
technology content.

Are You Part of the IT Crowd?

Connect with Pearson authors and editors via RSS feeds, Facebook,
Twitter, YouTube, and more! Visit **informit.com/socialconnect**.

 **inform IT.com** THE TRUSTED TECHNOLOGY LEARNING SOURCE PEARSON

↝Addison-Wesley **Cisco Press** EXAM/**CRAM** **IBM** Press. QUE PRENTICE HALL S**A**MS | Safari Books Online

Addison
Wesley

REGISTER

THIS PRODUCT

informit.com/register

Register the Addison-Wesley, Exam Cram, Prentice Hall, Que, and Sams products you own to unlock great benefits.

To begin the registration process, simply go to **informit.com/register** to sign in or create an account. You will then be prompted to enter the 10- or 13-digit ISBN that appears on the back cover of your product.

Registering your products can unlock the following benefits:

- Access to supplemental content, including bonus chapters, source code, or project files.
- A coupon to be used on your next purchase.

Registration benefits vary by product. Benefits will be listed on your Account page under Registered Products.

About InformIT – The Trusted Technology Learning Source

INFORMIT is home to the leading technology publishing imprints Addison-Wesley Professional, Cisco Press, Exam Cram, IBM Press, Prentice Hall Professional, Que, and Sams. Here you will gain access to quality and trusted content and resources from the authors, creators, innovators, and leaders of technology. Whether you're looking for a book on a new technology, a helpful article, timely newsletters, or access to the Safari Books Online digital library, InformIT has a solution for you.

informIT.com

THE TRUSTED TECHNOLOGY LEARNING SOURCE

Addison-Wesley | Cisco Press | Exam Cram | IBM Press
Que | Prentice Hall | Sams | VMware Press

SAFARI BOOKS ONLINE

ALWAYS LEARNING

PEARSON

The Essence

of Software

Engineering

Applying the SEMAT Kernel

Ivar Jacobson
Pan-Wei Ng
Paul E. McMahon
Ian Spence
Svante Lidman

✦✦Addison-Wesley

Upper Saddle River, NJ • Boston • Indianapolis • San Francisco
New York • Toronto • Montreal • London • Munich • Paris • Madrid
Capetown • Sydney • Tokyo • Singapore • Mexico City

Many of the designations used by manufacturers and sellers to distinguish their products are claimed as trademarks. Where those designations appear in this book, and the
publisher was aware of a trademark claim, the designations have been printed with initial
capital letters or in all capitals.

The authors and publisher have taken care in the preparation of this book, but make no
expressed or implied warranty of any kind and assume no responsibility for errors or omissions. No liability is assumed for incidental or consequential damages in connection with
or arising out of the use of the information or programs contained herein.

Figures P-1, P-2, P-3, 2-1, 3-1, 3-2, 3-4 and 22-2 are provided courtesy of the Software
Engineering Method and Theory (SEMAT) community.

The publisher offers excellent discounts on this book when ordered in quantity for bulk
purchases or special sales, which may include electronic versions and/or custom covers and
content particular to your business, training goals, marketing focus, and branding interests. For more information, please contact:

U.S. Corporate and Government Sales
(800) 382-3419
corpsales@pearsontechgroup.com

For sales outside the United States, please contact:

International Sales
international@pearsoned.com

Visit us on the Web: informit.com/aw

Cataloging-in-Publication Data is on file with the Library of Congress.

Copyright © 2013 Pearson Education, Inc.

All rights reserved. Printed in the United States of America. This publication is protected
by copyright, and permission must be obtained from the publisher prior to any prohibited
reproduction, storage in a retrieval system, or transmission in any form or by any means,
electronic, mechanical, photocopying, recording, or likewise. To obtain permission to use
material from this work, please submit a written request to Pearson Education, Inc., Per-
missions Department, One Lake Street, Upper Saddle River, New Jersey 07458, or you
may fax your request to (201) 236-3290.

ISBN-13: 978-0-321-88595-1
ISBN-10:   0-321-88595-3
Text printed in the United States on recycled paper at RR Donnelley in Crawfordsville,
Indiana.
First printing, January 2013

In every block of marble I see a statue as plain as though it stood before me, shaped and perfect in attitude and action. I have only to hew away the rough walls that imprison the lovely apparition to reveal it to the other eyes as mine see it.

—Michelangelo

Standing on the shoulders of a giant... We are liberating the essence from the burden of the whole.

—Ivar Jacobson

Contents

Foreword
by Robert Martin

The pendulum has swung again. This time it has swung toward craftsmanship. As one of the leaders of the craftsmanship movement, I think this is a good thing. I think it is important that software developers learn the pride of workmanship that is common in other crafts.

But when the pendulum swings, it often swings away from something else. And in this case it seems to be swinging away from the notion of engineering. The sentiment seems to be that if software is a craft, a kind of artistry, then it cannot be a science or an engineering discipline. I disagree with this rather strenuously.

Software is both a craft and a science, both a work of passion and a work of principle. Writing good software requires both wild flights of imagination and creativity, as well as the hard reality of engineering tradeoffs. Software, like any other worthwhile human endeavor, is a hybrid between the left and right brain.

This book is an attempt at describing that balance. It proposes a software engineering framework or *kernel* that meets the need for engineering discipline, while at the same time leaving the development space open for the creativity and emergent behavior needed for a craft.

Most software process descriptions use an assembly line metaphor. The project moves from position to position along the line until it is complete. The prototypical process of this type is the waterfall, in which the project moves from Analysis to Design to Implementation. In RUP the project moves from Inception to Elaboration to Construction to Transition.

The kernel in this book represents a software development effort as a continuously operating abstract mechanism composed of components and relationships. The project does not move from position to position within this mechanism as in the assembly line metaphor. Rather, there is a continuous flow through the mechanism as opportunities are transformed into requirements, and then into code and tests, and then into deployments.

The state of that mechanism is exposed through a set of critical indicators, called *alphas,* which represent how well the underlying components are functioning. These alphas progress from state to state through a sequence of actions taken by the development team in response to the current states.

As the project progresses, the environment will change, the needs of the customer will shift, the team will evolve, and the mechanism will get out of kilter. The team will have to take further actions to tune the mechanism to get it back into proper operation.

This metaphor of a continuous mechanism, as opposed to an assembly line, is driven by the agile worldview. Agile projects do not progress through phases. Rather, they operate in a manner that continuously transforms customer needs into software solutions. But agile projects can get out of kilter. They might get into a mode where they aren't refactoring enough, or they are pairing too much, or their estimates are unreliable, or their customers aren't engaged.

The kernel in this book describes the critical indicators and actions that allow such malfunctions to be detected and then corrected. Teams can use it to tune their behaviors, communications, workflows, and work products in order to keep the machine running smoothly and predictably.

The central theme of the book is excellent. The notion of the alphas, states, and actions is compelling, simple, and effective. It's just the right kind of idea for a kernel. I think it is an idea that could help the whole software community.

If you are deeply interested in software process and engineering, if you are a manager or team leader who needs to keep the development organization running like a well-oiled machine, or if you are a CTO in search of some science that can help you understand your development organizations, then I think you'll find this book very interesting.

After reading the book, I found myself wanting to get my hands on a deck of cards so that I could look through them and play with them.

—Robert Martin
 (unclebob)
 February 2012

Foreword
by Bertrand Meyer

Software projects everywhere look for methodology and are not finding it. They do, fortunately, find individual practices that suit them; but when it comes to identifying a coherent set of practices that can guide a project from start to finish, they are too often confronted with dogmatic compendiums that are too rigid for their needs. A method should be adaptable to every project's special circumstances: it should be backed by strong, objective arguments; and it should make it possible to track the benefits.

The work of Ivar Jacobson and his colleagues, started as part of the SEMAT initiative, has taken a systematic approach to identifying a "kernel" of software engineering principles and practices that have stood the test of time and recognition. Building on this theoretical effort, they describe project development in terms of states and alphas. It is essential for the project leaders and the project members to know, at every point in time, what is the current state of the project. This global state, however, is a combination of the states of many diverse components of the system; the term *alpha* covers such individual components. An alpha can be a software artifact, like the requirements or the code; a human element, like the project team; or a pure abstraction, like the opportunity that led to the idea of a project. Every alpha has, at a particular time, a state; combining all these alpha states defines the state of the project. Proper project management and success requires knowing this state at every stage of development.

The role of the kernel is to identify the key alphas of software development and, for each of them, to identify the standard states through which it can evolve. For example, an opportunity will progress through the states Identified, Solution Needed, Value Established, Viable, Addressed, and Benefits Accrued. Other alphas have similarly standardized sets of states.

The main value of this book is in the identification of these fundamental alphas and their states, enabling an engineering approach in which the project has a clear view of where it stands through a standardized set of controls.

The approach is open, since it does not prescribe any particular practice but instead makes it possible to integrate many different practices, which do not even have to come from the same methodological source—like some agile variant—but can combine good ideas from different sources. A number of case studies illustrate how to apply the ideas in practice.

Software practitioners and teachers of software engineering are in dire need of well-grounded methodological work. This book provides a solid basis for anyone interested in turning software project development into a solid discipline with a sound engineering basis.

—Bertrand Meyer
March 2012

Foreword
by Richard Soley

Software runs our world; *software-intensive systems,* as Grady Booch calls them, are the core structure that drives equity and derivative trading, communications, logistics, government services, management of great national and international military organizations, and medical systems—and even allows elementary school teacher Mr. Smith to send homework assignments to little Susie. Even mechanical systems have given way to software-driven systems (think of fly-by-wire aircraft, for example); the trend is not slowing, but accelerating. We depend on software, and often we depend on it for our very lives. Amazingly, more often than not software development resembles an artist's craft far more than an engineering discipline.

Did you ever wonder how the architects and builders of the great, ancient temples of Egypt or Greece knew how to build grand structures that would stand the test of time, surviving hundreds, or even thousands of years, through earthquakes, wars, and weather? The Egyptians had amazing mathematical abilities for their time, but triangulation was just about the top of their technical acumen. The reality, of course, is that luck has more to do with the survival of the great façade of the Celsus Library of Ephesus, in present-day Selçuk, Turkey, than any tremendous ability to understand construction for the ages.

This, of course, is no longer the case. Construction is now *civil engineering,* and civil engineering is an engineering discipline. No one would ever consider going back to the old hand-designed, hand-built, and far more dangerous structures of the distant past. Buildings still fail in the face of powerful weather phenomena, but not at anywhere near the rate they did 500 years ago.

What an odd dichotomy, then, that in the design of some large, complex systems we depend on a clear engineering methodology, but in the development of certain other large, complex systems we are quite content to depend on the ad hoc, handmade work of artisans. To be sure, that's not always the case; quite often, stricter processes and analytics are used to build software for software-intensive systems that "cannot" fail, where more time and money is available for their construction; aircraft avionics and other *embedded* systems design is often far more rigorous (and costly) than desktop computing software.

Really, this is more of a measure of the youth of the computing field than anything else, and the youth of our field is never more evident than in the lack of a grand unifying theory to underpin the software development process. How can we expect the computing field to have consistent software development processes, consistently taught at universities worldwide, consistently supported by software development organizations, and consistently delivered by software development teams, when we don't have a globally shared language that defines the software development process?

It is worth noting, however, that there is more than one way to build a building and more than one way to construct software. So the language or languages we need should define quarks and atoms instead of molecules—atomic and subatomic parts that we can mix and match to define, carry out, measure, and improve the software development process itself. We can expect the software development world to fight on about agile versus non-agile development, and traditional team-member programming versus pair programming, for years to come; but we should demand and expect that the process building blocks we choose can be consistently applied, matched, and compared as necessary, and measured for efficacy. That core process design language is called *Essence*. Note that, in fact, in this book there is a "kernel" of design primitives that are themselves defined in a common language; I will leave this complication for the authors to explain in detail.

In late 2009, Ivar Jacobson, Bertrand Meyer, and I came together to clarify the need for a widely accepted process design kernel and language and to build an international team to address that need. The three of us came from quite different backgrounds in the software world, but all of us have spent time in the trenches slinging code, all of us have led software development teams, and all of us have tried to address the software complexity problem in various ways. Our analogies have differed (operatic ones being quite noticeably Prof. Meyer's), our team leadership styles have differed, and our starting points have been quite visibly different. These differences, however, led to an outstanding international cooperation called Software Engineering Method and Theory, or SEMAT. The Essence kernel, a major Object Management Group (OMG) standards process, and this book are outputs of this cooperative project.

Around us a superb team of great thinkers formed, meeting for the first time at ETH in Zürich two years ago, with other meetings soon afterward. That team has struggled to bring together diverse experiences and worldviews into a core kernel composed of atomic parts that can be mixed and matched, connected as needed, drawn on a blueprint, analyzed, and put into practice to define, hire, direct, and measure real development teams. As I write this, the OMG is considering how to capture the work of this team as an international software development standard. It's an exciting time to be in the software world, as we transition from groups of artisans sometimes working together effectively, to engineers using well-defined, measured, and consistent construction practices to build software that works.

The software development industry needs and demands a core kernel and language for defining software development practices—practices that can be mixed and matched, brought on board from other organizations, measured, integrated, and compared and contrasted for speed, quality, and price. Soon we'll stop delivering software by hand; soon our great software edifices will stop falling down. SEMAT and Essence may not be the end of that journey to developing an engineering culture for software, and they certainly don't represent the first attempt to do so; but they stand a strong chance of delivering broad acceptance in the software world. This thoughtful book gives a good grounding in ways to think about the problem, and a language to address the need; every software *engineer* should read it.

—Richard Mark Soley, Ph.D.
  38,000 feet over the Pacific Ocean
  March 2012

Preface

Everyone who develops software knows that it is a complex and risky business, and is always on the lookout for new ideas that will help him or her develop better software. Luckily, software engineering is still a young and growing profession—one that sees new innovations and improvements in best practices every year. These new ideas are essential to the growth of our industry—just look at the improvements and benefits that lean and agile thinking have brought to software development teams.

Successful software development teams need to strike a balance between quickly delivering working software systems, satisfying their stakeholders, addressing their risks, and improving their way of working. For that, they need an effective thinking framework—one that bridges the gap between their current way of working and any new ideas they want to take on board. This book presents such a thinking framework in the form of an actionable kernel—something we believe will benefit any team wishing to balance their risks and improve their way of working.

INSPIRATION

This book was inspired by, and is a direct response to, the SEMAT Call for Action. It is, in its own way, one small step in the process to refound software engineering.

SEMAT (Software Engineering Method and Theory) was founded in September 2009 by Ivar Jacobson, Bertrand Meyer, and Richard Soley, who felt the time had come to fundamentally change the way people work with software development methods. Together they wrote a call for action, which in a few lines

Software engineering is gravely hampered today by immature practices. Specific problems include:

- The prevalence of fads more typical of a fashion industry than of an engineering discipline
- The lack of a sound, widely accepted theoretical basis
- The huge number of methods and method variants, with differences little understood and artificially magnified
- The lack of credible experimental evaluation and validation
- The split between industry practice and academic research

We support a process to refound software engineering based on a solid theory, proven principles and best practices that:

- Include a kernel of widely-agreed elements, extensible for specific uses
- Address both technology and people issues
- Are supported by industry, academia, researchers and users
- Support extension in the face of changing requirements and technology

Figure P-1 Excerpt from the SEMAT Call for Action

identifies a number of critical problems with current software engineering practice, explains why there is a need to act, and suggests what needs to be done. Figure P-1 is an excerpt from the SEMAT Call for Action.

The call for action received a broad base of support, including a growing list of signatories and supporters.[1] The call for action's assertion that the software industry is prone to fads and fashions has led some people to assume that SEMAT and its supporters are resistant to new ideas. This could not be further from the truth. As you will see in this book, they are very keen on new ideas—in fact, this book is all about some of the new ideas coming from SEMAT itself. What SEMAT and its supporters are against is the non-lean, non-agile behavior that comes from

---

1. The current list can be found at www.semat.org.

people adopting inappropriate solutions just because they believe these solutions are fashionable, or because of peer pressure or political correctness.

In February 2010 the founders developed the call for action into a vision statement.[2] In accordance with this vision SEMAT then focused on two major goals:

1. Finding a kernel of widely agreed-on elements
2. Defining a solid theoretical basis

To a large extent these two tasks are independent of each other. Finding the kernel and its elements is a pragmatic exercise requiring people with long experience in software development and knowledge of many of the existing methods. Defining the theoretical basis requires academic research and may take many years to reach a successful outcome.

THE POWER OF THE COMMON GROUND

SEMAT's first step was to identify a common ground for software engineering. This common ground is manifested as a kernel of essential elements that are universal to all software development efforts, and a simple language for describing methods and practices. This book provides an introduction to the SEMAT kernel, and how to use it when developing software and communicating between teams and team members. It is a book for software professionals, not methodologists. It will make use of the language but will not dwell on it or describe it in detail.

The kernel was first published in the SEMAT OMG Submission.[3] As shown in Figures P-2 and P-3, the kernel contains a

---

2. The SEMAT Vision statement can be found at the SEMAT website, www.semat.org.

3. "Essence – Kernel and Language for Software Engineering Methods." Available from www.semat.org.

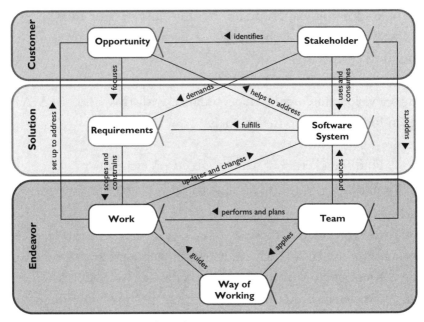

Figure P-2 Things to work with

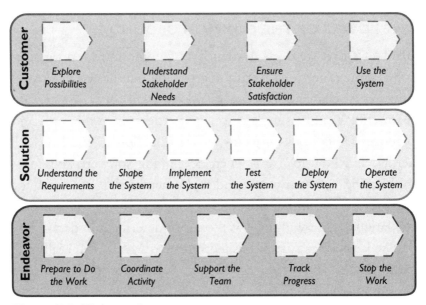

Figure P-3 Things to do

small number of "things we always work with" and "things we always do" when developing software systems. There is also work that is ongoing, with the goal of defining the "skills we always need to have," but this will have to wait until future versions of the kernel and is outside the scope of this book.[4]

We won't delve into the details of the kernel here as this is the subject of Part I, but it is worth taking a few moments to think about why it is so important to establish the common ground in this way. More than just a conceptual model, as you will see through the practical examples in this book, the kernel provides

- A thinking framework for teams to reason about the progress they are making and the health of their endeavors
- A framework for teams to assemble and continuously improve their way of working
- A common ground for improved communication, standardized measurement, and the sharing of best practices
- A foundation for accessible, interoperable method and practice definitions
- And most importantly, a way to help teams understand where they are and what they should do next

THE BIG IDEA

What makes the kernel anything more than just a conceptual model of software engineering? What is really new here? This can be summarized into the three guiding principles shown in Figure P-4.

---

4. A kernel with similar properties as the SEMAT kernel was first developed at Ivar Jacobson International in 2006 (www.ivarjacobson.com). This kernel has served as an inspiration and an experience base for the work on the SEMAT kernel.

Figure P-4 Guiding principles of the kernel

The Kernel Is Actionable

A unique feature of the kernel is how the "things to work with" are handled. These are captured as alphas rather than work products (such as documents). An alpha is an essential element of the software engineering endeavor, one that is relevant to an assessment of its progress and health. As shown in Figure P-2, SEMAT has identified seven alphas: Opportunity, Stakeholders, Requirements, Software System, Work, Way of Working, and Team. The alphas are characterized by a simple set of states that represent their progress and health. As an example, the Software System moves through the states of Architecture Selected, Demonstrable, Usable, Ready, Operational, and Retired. Each state has a checklist that specifies the criteria needed to reach the state. It is these states that make the kernel actionable and enable it to guide the behavior of software development teams.

The kernel presents software development not as a linear process but as a network of collaborating elements; elements that need to be balanced and maintained to allow teams to progress effectively and efficiently, eliminate waste, and develop great software. The alphas in the kernel provide an overall framework for driving and progressing software development efforts, regardless of the practices applied or the software development philosophy followed.

As practices are added to the kernel, additional alphas will be added to represent the things that either drive the progress of the kernel alphas, or inhibit and prevent progress from being made. For example, the Requirements will not be addressed as a whole but will be progressed requirement item by requirement item. It is the progress of the individual requirement items that will drive or inhibit the progress and health of the Requirements. The requirement items could be of many different types—for example, they could be features, user stories, or use-case slices, all of which can be represented as alphas and have their state tracked. The benefit of relating these smaller items to the coarser-grained kernel elements is that it allows the tracking of the health of the endeavor as a whole. This provides a necessary balance to the lower-level tracking of the individual items, enabling teams to understand and optimize their way of working.

The Kernel Is Extensible

Another unique feature of the kernel is the way it can be extended to support different kinds of development (e.g., new development, legacy enhancements, in-house development, offshore, software product lines, etc.). The kernel allows you to add practices, such as user stories, use cases, component-based development, architecture, pair programming, daily stand-up meetings, self-organizing teams, and so on, to build the methods you need. For example, different methods could be assembled for in-house and outsourced development, or for the development of safety-critical embedded systems and back office reporting systems.

The key idea here is that of practice separation. While the term *practice* has been widely used in the industry for many years, the kernel has a specific approach to the handling and sharing of practices. Practices are presented as distinct, separate, modular units, which a team can choose to use or not to use. This contrasts with traditional approaches that treat software development as a soup of indistinguishable practices and lead teams to dump the good with the bad when they move from one method to another.

The Kernel Is Practical

Perhaps the most important feature of the kernel is the way it is used in practice. Traditional approaches to software development methods tend to focus on supporting process engineers or quality engineers. The kernel, in contrast, is a hands-on, tangible thinking framework focused on supporting software professionals as they carry out their work.

For example, the kernel can be touched and used through the use of cards (see Figure P-5). The cards provide concise reminders and cues for team members as they go about their daily tasks. By providing practical checklists and prompts, as opposed to conceptual discussions, the kernel becomes something the team uses on a daily basis. This is a fundamental difference from

Figure P-5 Cards make the kernel tangible.

traditional approaches, which tend to overemphasize method description as opposed to method use and tend to only be consulted by people new to the team.

THE KERNEL IN ACTION

Although the ideas in this book will be new to many of you, they have already been successfully applied in both industry and academia.

Early adopters of the kernel idea[5] include the following.

- MunichRe, the world's leading reinsurance company, where a family of "collaboration models" have been assembled to cover the whole spectrum of software and application work. Four collaboration models have been built on the same kernel from the same set of 12 practices. The models are Exploratory, Standard, Maintenance, and Support.

- Fujitsu Services, where the Apt Toolkit has been built on top of an early version of the software engineering kernel, including both agile and waterfall ways of working.

- A major Japanese consumer electronics company, whose software processes have been defined on top of an early version of the kernel, allowing the company to help teams apply new practices and manage their offshore development vendor.

- KPN, where a kernel-based process was adopted by more than 300 projects across 13 programs as part of a move to iterative development. The kernel also provided the basis for a new result-focused QA process, which could be applied to all projects regardless of the method or practices used.

---

5. In all cases they used the kernel and practices developed by Ivar Jacobson International.

- A major UK government department, where a kernel-based agile toolset was introduced to enable disciplined agility and the tracking of project progress and health in a practice-independent fashion.

The kernel is already being used in first- and second-year software engineering courses at KTH Royal Institute of Technology in Sweden.

- The first-year courses were run by Anders Sjögren. After the students conducted their projects, Anders and the students went through the SEMAT alphas and matched them to their project results. Here, the students had the opportunity to acquaint themselves with and evaluate the alphas as well as gain insight into the project's progress and health.

- The second-year courses were run by Mira Kajko-Mattsson. Here, the students were requested to actively use the SEMAT kernel when running their projects along with the development method they followed. Mira created an example software development scenario and evaluated the scenario for each alpha, its states, and the state checklist items. The students were then requested to do the same when conducting and evaluating their projects.

The courses taught the students the following lessons.

- The kernel assures that all the essential aspects of software engineering are considered in a project. By matching the project results against the kernel alphas, the students can easily identify the good and bad sides of their development methods.

- The kernel prepares students for future software engineering endeavors with minimal teaching effort. Because they had to follow all the kernel alphas, the students could learn the total scope of the software engineering endeavor and thereby know what will be required of them in their professional careers.

HOW DOES THE KERNEL RELATE TO AGILE AND OTHER EXISTING APPROACHES?

The kernel can be used with all the currently popular management and technical practices, including Scrum, Kanban, risk-driven iterative, waterfall, use-case-driven development, acceptance-test-driven development, continuous integration, test-driven development, and so on. It will help teams embarking on the development of new and innovative software products and teams involved in enhancing and maintaining mature and established software products. It will help teams of all sizes from one-man bands to thousand-strong software engineering programs.

For example, the kernel supports the values of the Agile Manifesto. With its focus on checklists and results, and its inherent practice independence, it values individuals and interactions over processes and tools. With its focus on the needs of professional software development teams, it values teams working and fulfilling team responsibilities over the following methods.

The kernel doesn't in any way compete with existing methods, be they agile or anything else. On the contrary, the kernel is agnostic to a team's chosen method. Even if you have already chosen, or are using, a particular method the kernel can still help you. Regardless of the method used, as Robert Martin has pointed out in his Foreword to this book, projects—even agile ones—can get out of kilter, and when they do teams need to know more. This is where the real value of the kernel can be found. It can guide a team in the actions to take to get back on course, to extend their method, or to address a critical gap in their way of working. At all times it focuses on the needs of the software professional and values the "use of methods" over the "description of method definitions" (as has been normal in the past).

The kernel doesn't just support modern best practices. It also recognizes that a vast amount of software is already developed and needs to be maintained; it will live for decades and it will have to be maintained in an efficient way. This means the way you work with this software will have to evolve alongside the software itself. New practices will need to be introduced in a way that complements the ones already in use. The kernel provides the mechanisms to migrate legacy methods from monolithic waterfall approaches to more modern agile ones and beyond, in an evolutionary way. It allows you to change your legacy methods practice by practice while maintaining and improving the team's ability to deliver.

HOW THE KERNEL WILL HELP YOU

Use of the kernel has many benefits for you as an experienced or aspiring software professional, and for the teams you work in. For example, it provides guidance to help you assess the progress and health of your software development endeavors, evaluate your current practices, and improve your way of working. It will also help you to improve communication, move more easily between teams, and adopt new ideas. And it will help the industry as a whole by improving interoperability between teams, suppliers, and development organizations.

By providing a practice-independent foundation for the definition of software methods, the kernel also has the power to completely transform the way methods are defined and practices are shared. For example, by allowing teams to mix and match practices from different sources to build and improve their way of working, the kernel addresses two of the key methodological problems facing the industry.

1. Teams are no longer trapped by their methods. They can continuously improve their way of working by adding or removing practices as and when their situation demands.
2. Methodologists no longer need to waste their time describing complete methods. They can easily describe their new ideas in a concise and reusable way.

Finally, there are also benefits for academia, particularly in the areas of education and research. The kernel will provide a basis for the creation of foundation courses in software engineering, ones that can then be complemented with additional courses in specific practices—either as part of the initial educational curriculum or later during the student's further professional development. Equally as important is the kernel's ability to act as a shared reference model and enabler for further research and experimentation

HOW TO READ THIS BOOK

This book is intended for anyone who wants to have a clear frame of reference when developing software, researching software development, or sharing software development experiences.

For software professionals the goal of this book is to show how the kernel can help solve challenges you face every day when doing your job. It demonstrates how the kernel is used in different situations from small-scale development to large-scale development.

For students and other aspiring software professionals, the goal of the book is to illustrate some of the challenges software professionals face and how to deal with them. It will provide you with a firm foundation for further study and help you learn what you otherwise only learn through experience.

The book is organized to allow gradual learning, and concepts are introduced and illustrated incrementally. We hope this book will be useful to software professionals, educators, and students, and we look forward to your feedback.

The book is structured into seven short parts.

Part I: The Kernel Idea Explained

An overview of the kernel with examples of how it can be used in practice.

Part II: Using the Kernel to Run an Iteration

A walkthrough of how the kernel can be used to run an iteration.

Part III: Using the Kernel to Run a Software Endeavor

A description of how you can use the kernel to run a complete software endeavor—for example, a project of some size—from idea to production.

Part IV: Scaling Development with the Kernel

A demonstration of how the kernel is flexible in supporting different practices, organizations, and domains.

Part V: How the Kernel Changes the Way You Work with Methods

Takes a step back and discusses the principles for you to apply the kernel effectively and successfully to your specific situation.

Part VI: What's Really New Here?

A summary of the highlights and key differentiators of SEMAT and this book.

Part VII: Epilogue

A forward-looking discussion of how we can get even more value from the kernel in the future.

FURTHER READING

Jacobson, I., and B. Meyer. 2009. Methods need theory. *Dr. Dobb's Journal.*

Jacobson I., and I. Spence. 2009. Why we need a theory for software engineering. Dr. Dobb's Journal.

Jacobson I., B. Meyer, and R. Soley. 2009. Call for Action: The Semat Initiative. Dr. Dobb's Journal.

Jacobson I., B. Meyer, and R. Soley. 2009. The Semat Vision Statement.

Fujitsu, Ivar Jacobson International AB, Model Driven Solutions. 2012. Essence – Kernel and Language for Software Engineering Methods. Initial Submission – Version 1.0.

OMG. 2012. Request for Proposal (RFP). A Foundation for the Agile Creation and Enactment of Software Engineering Methods. OMG.

Jacobson I., P.W. Ng, and I. Spence. 2007. Enough of Processes: Let's Do Practices. *Journal of Object Technology* 6(6):41–67.

Ng P.W., and M. Magee. Light Weight Application Lifecycle Management Using State-Cards. *Agile Journal,* October 10, 2010.

Azoff, M. EssWork 3.0 and Essential Practices 4.0. Ivar Jacobson International. OVUM Technology Report, Reference Code TA001906ADT. April 2012.

Azoff, M. Apt Methods and Tools. Fujitsu. OVUM Technology Report, Reference Code O100032-002. January 2011.

Acknowledgments

We wish to acknowledge and thank the contributors to SEMAT, in particular (alphabetically): Jakob Axelsson, Stefan Bylund, Bob Corrick, Michael Goedicke, Lulu He, Shihong Huang, Carlos Mario Zapata Jaramillo, Mira Kajko-Mattsson, Philippe Kruchten, Bruce Macisaac, Winifred Menezes, Richard Murphy, Hanna Oktaba, Roland Racko, Ed Seidewitz, and Michael Strieve.

PART I
THE KERNEL IDEA EXPLAINED

In the first part of the book, we present the kernel and the ideas behind the kernel in a nutshell. We first demonstrate, through a simple story, how a software professional (Smith) helps a team address some software development challenges by using the kernel. Using this story we introduce the concepts behind the kernel, how we made the kernel tangible for software professionals, and how to extend the kernel to cover a broad range of software development challenges through practices. Through this, we demonstrate how the kernel helps you develop software, grow and scale to a large development, learn new practices, and evolve your way of working.

1

A Glimpse of How the Kernel Can Be Used

Being a member of a team developing software is very engaging. You are creative, solve hard problems, and collaborate with customers and colleagues. The sense of pride shared in the team when you deliver a high-quality piece of software and get praise by end users is truly rewarding. But why can't it be like that more often?

Even if most software professionals aspire to be part of this kind of tight-knit, creative, and focused team, they often face obstacles that make it difficult. Let's hear what some of them have to say about their challenges.

Fred: "The requirements go in different directions, so our work is not converging on anything that can be released."

Eric: "The proposed software architecture doesn't seem to solve the right problems, but I don't know how to drive it forward."

Susan: "Management is panicking and throwing more developers on the team, but we already have difficulty coordinating the existing team members."

Steve: "I have to spend a lot of time pretending I am following the mandated development process and producing documentation that isn't really useful for anyone."

These are just some of the challenges and frustrations Fred, Eric, Susan, and Steve are facing.

What can we do to help them?

1.1 WHY IS DEVELOPING GOOD SOFTWARE SO CHALLENGING?

If you have been involved with developing software for some time, you have most certainly experienced how complex it can be. But *why* is it so complex?

- **It is multidimensional.** First, challenges can come in any dimension: requirements, architecture, teamwork, competency, and so on. For example, Fred is having problems with requirements, and Susan is facing problems with team organization and, of course, with the way management is acting. These dimensions are not independent of one another, so to be successful you need to deal with them simultaneously.

- **It requires competent individuals.** Fred needs to help the customer understand what is needed. The customer representative, Angela, likes to have someone to bounce ideas off of to help her clarify her thoughts as she tries to get the requirements to converge. This requires communication skills and requirements collaboration skills from Fred. And it is not just about requirements and communication. Together, the team needs to have competencies covering all dimensions of the endeavor: architecture, test, and so on.

- **It is a team sport.** The creation of good software is a collective intellectual achievement, and to create nontrivial software good collaboration is essential. It is not enough that Fred knows how to handle the requirements challenge. His team needs to understand things, too, and so do his customer representative, Angela, and his management. In general, they have to know what is most important to work on as a team.

So far, we have not reached a solution to the challenges faced by Fred, Eric, Susan, and Steve. But we know we need to address the three main characteristics of software development: (1) multidimensional challenges, (2) competency, and (3) teamwork.

1.2 GETTING TO THE ESSENCE OF SOFTWARE ENGINEERING: THE KERNEL

So, what answer shall we give Fred, Eric, Susan, and Steve? It is really to focus on the essentials. Get the basics right, make sure you have the right knowledge, and collaborate to get the job done. But this needs to be made concrete, and this is precisely what the kernel does—it makes the essence of software development concrete. The kernel comprises a number of things that together capture the essence of software engineering and provide practical guidance for the likes of Fred, Eric, Susan, and Steve.

- The kernel identifies several areas of a software endeavor that a team must be mindful of and assess for progress and health. These include the Requirements, Opportunity, Stakeholders, Team, Work, Way of Working, and, of course, Software System to be delivered. The kernel identifies states for each of these as a guide for how to work with them effectively.

- The kernel raises the visibility of which competencies a team needs in order to successfully carry out a software endeavor.

- The kernel identifies the kinds of things you need to attend to in order to achieve progress and health in a software endeavor.

These things that the kernel identifies will help you to resolve typical challenges of software development.

1.3 USING THE KERNEL TO ADDRESS SPECIFIC CHALLENGES: AN EXAMPLE

To appreciate the usefulness of the kernel, let's discuss Fred's situation. Recall that Fred and Angela had problems with requirements going in different directions. Now, Smith, a more experienced colleague of Fred and Angela, was asked to help. The following discussion demonstrates how Smith, through the kernel, worked with Fred and Angela to resolve the challenge. In the following text, the words in *italics* come from the kernel. In this chapter we will use them informally first, and after walking through the conversations among Fred, Angela, and Smith we will take a step back and discuss what the words in italics really stand for.

1.3.1 Getting to the Heart of the Problem

The first thing, which Smith needed to do, was to understand why things were going in different directions and the impact this was having. So Smith started asking questions as follows.

- *Opportunity:* The system, which Fred was working on, was intended to meet a business need or opportunity. What was that need? The system must provide some value. What was that value? If this value was not understood, then debating detailed requirements would not help.

- *Stakeholders:* Was Fred getting information from the right stakeholders? Were the stakeholders engaged and really thinking about requirements? Were the stakeholders in agreement? Specifically, did Angela have the required knowledge of the system and its users to represent them? In other words, was Angela able to make sound decisions on the scope of the system?

- *Requirements:* Did Fred have a clear understanding of the scope of the system and its requirements? Did he have a good understanding of business as well as technical risks? Was he focusing on the requirements in the right order? Was he trying to get too many requirements nailed down up front?

- *Software System:* Are the requirements going in different directions because the stakeholders do not have a good understanding of the capabilities and limitations of the existing software system? Are the system and its architecture robust in the face of change? Is this a requirements problem, or a design problem?

- *Team:* Were Fred and his teammates collaborating to design a robust system, a system that is easy to extend? Did the team have the competence to get the job done? Was the team working together as a unit, or were there conflicts waiting to surface?

- *Work:* Were the problems being caused by the need to find work for all the team members, or because of the way the work had been planned? Was the team working on the wrong things because of a previous planning error?

- *Way of Working:* Were the problems being caused by the way the team worked and the method they were following? Were the requirements diverging because the method being followed insisted that all the requirements were detailed before any design or coding could take place?

Through the conversation with Fred, Smith discovered the key problem was that Fred was not working on the right subset of the requirements. Smith used a way to classify requirements according to their value to customers and stakeholders, and whether there is a shared understanding between the team and stakeholders. This is captured in Figure 1-1, which Smith presented to Fred and Angela.

Fred was building software for a mobile device. Some parts were about enhancing existing capabilities (e.g., better sound and video quality, better connectivity to social networks) and those parts were clear and mapped to quadrant A in Figure 1-1. There were other parts, which Angela called Value Added Services. Angela hadn't gotten her head around the theme behind this Value Added Services part, let alone the individual requirement items for it. Angela was also a busy person and only available once in a while, which made communication and feedback challenging. Thus, Value Added Services mapped to quadrant C.

During this period, the team spent more time discussing what the system could do than what the system must do. In other words, they had trouble staying focused on their immediate goal. Also, instead of completing those requirements that were clear and of high priority they were trying to complete the

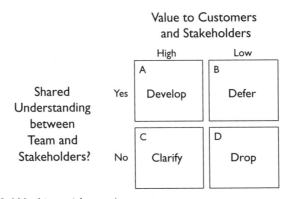

Figure 1-1 Working with requirement

requirements that were least understood. Hence, Fred and his teammates could not converge on anything.

1.3.2 Addressing the Challenge

Having recognized why Fred and his team had challenges with requirements, Smith, Fred, and Angela could start to devise a strategy to deal with the situation.

They agreed that for those requirements that were clear and of high priority, they would follow their current approach. Fred and his teammates could start coding and rapidly demonstrate results.

They also agreed that for those requirements that were of high priority and unclear, an alternate approach was needed. They agreed that implementing such requirements fully in executable code would be too wasteful. Instead, they planned separate activities to clarify what Value Added Services meant.

- *Explore Possibilities.* The *opportunity* is the reason for the production of the new, or changed, *software system.* Fred and Angela had to understand the need for the Value Added Services and make sure that for this *opportunity* there was clear *value established.*

- *Understand Requirements.* Once the value of the *opportunity* is established, Fred and Angela need to first get the *requirements* for the Value Added Services *bounded;* only then would the team be able to start to spike[1] the most important *requirements* to drive further clarification. Smith recommended walking through end-user scenarios as a means to get the *requirements bounded.*

---

1. A *spike* is a timeboxed period of research and development to research a concept and/or create a prototype, or a preliminary solution. The main goal of a spike is to gain knowledge as opposed to completing a set of requirements.

- *Shape the System.* Fred's team could then implement the *software system* and make it *demonstrable*. This would enable them to confirm with Angela that they were on the right track.

Angela as a customer representative represents the *stakeholders* and manages the scope of the *software system*. To be successful, Angela needed help to explore the *opportunity*. Fred and Angela weren't quite sure they had the right skills, so they asked Smith to help them.

In the beginning, the work progressed slowly as they tried to understand the *opportunity* and identify a first set of *requirements*. Smith had to guide Fred and Angela to focus on the right things. Gradually, Fred and Angela understood. Angela brought in other people to join the discussions and Fred involved his teammates. So the *team* met their challenge by *collaborating*, and eventually their views started to converge.

1.4 LEARNING HOW TO ADDRESS DEVELOPMENT CHALLENGES WITH THE KERNEL

Smith was quick to find the root causes of Fred's requirements challenge. But how did Smith do it? What knowledge and experience did he use?

If you are good at helping struggling software teams, you know instinctively how to do what Smith did. You know the things to look for, how to ask the right questions without offending Fred and Angela, and how to guide them to a solution. You can see what is sound and what is not and you have skills to help others see that, too. You have everything you need in your head and don't need anything more.

Sound instincts are great, but most people benefit from having some thinking tools when reasoning about challenges and potential solutions. This is where the kernel can help.

In our earlier discussion about Fred's challenges, we used italicized words and phrases to indicate concepts from the kernel. This illustrates the following.

- The kernel provides a frame of reference when thinking about software development challenges.
- If you and your teammates have a common understanding of these concepts, you will communicate better.

In the next chapter we will build on this informal introduction and look at the kernel in more detail.

2

A Little More Detail about the Kernel

The kernel captures a set of concepts that are essential to the success of any software endeavor. It helps you to communicate effectively with your fellow teammates, overcome challenges, and run your software endeavor effectively. These concepts are not radically new but they are intuitive to software professionals. What the kernel does is bring the concepts together in a concise manner so that you can make effective use of them. In the following two chapters we will take a closer look at the kernel and what is in it. In this chapter we will look at how the kernel helped the team in Chapter 1, and in Chapter 3 we will provide a high-level view of the entire kernel.

2.1 HOW TO USE THE KERNEL TO ADDRESS A SPECIFIC CHALLENGE: AN EXAMPLE

In the preceding chapter we showed how Smith was able to find the root cause of the team's requirements challenge and come to a solution quickly. How did he do that? He used a number of concepts from the kernel, alphas and states, marked in *italics* in that chapter. In this chapter we will go through these words and phrases and describe what they mean.

Smith only used part of the kernel, so in this chapter we will only discuss this part. The kernel can also be used to address challenges with architecture, testing, managing your work, and so on. Chapter 3 provides an overview of the complete kernel.

2.2 INTRODUCING THE ALPHAS

Alphas are subjects in a software endeavor whose evolution we want to understand, monitor, direct, and control. We already introduced a number of alphas, such as Opportunity, Stakeholders, Requirements, Software System, and Team, all of which Smith used.

Definition

Alphas represent the things you need to monitor for progress and health to steer your endeavor to a successful conclusion, and they have states and checklists to that effect. A good way to remember this is as a mnemonic formed from the words "Aspiration Led Progress and Health Attribute," which stresses that (1) alphas are about progress and health, (2) they are focused on achieving positive results, and (3) they should be looked at as a set and not individually.

Alphas exist regardless of their concrete representation. There will always be requirements, regardless of whether you document them or not, or how you document them (e.g., as user stories, features, use cases, etc.). Similarly, there will always be a software system regardless of the techniques used and documents produced. Simply put, alphas are the most important things you must tend to in order to be successful in a software development endeavor.

The alphas that Smith used are shown in Figure 2-1, denoted by a stylized Greek alpha character. They are described in the list that follows.

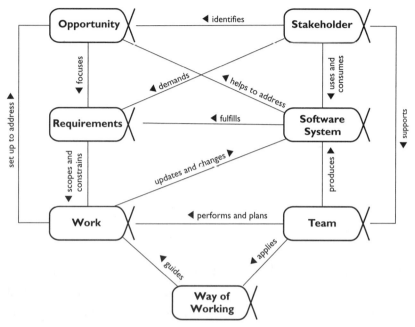

Figure 2-1 Alphas that Smith used to discuss changing requirement

- *Opportunity:* The set of circumstances that makes it appropriate to develop or change a software system.

- *Stakeholders:* The people, groups, or organizations that affect or are affected by a software system.

- *Requirements:* What the software system must do to address the opportunity and satisfy the stakeholders.

- *Software System:* A system made up of software, hardware, and data that provides its primary value by the execution of the software.

- *Team:* The group of people actively engaged in the development, maintenance, delivery, and support of a specific software system.

- *Work:* Activity involving mental or physical effort done in order to achieve a result.

- *Way of Working:* The tailored set of practices and tools used by a team to guide and support their work.

As illustrated in Figure 2-1, there are relationships between alphas that indicate how problems in one dimension can affect another. Smith used these relationships to explore the root causes for the requirements problem in Fred's case. One root cause he identified was that Fred's team tried to create complete implementations for the least understood requirements as opposed to clarifying them through a mix of workshops, spikes, and incremental implementation and feedback.

Now, to do well in a software endeavor your Opportunity must be good, your Requirements must be good, your Stakeholders must be good, your Software System must be good, and your Team must be good. How do you know if they are good? Associated with each alpha is a set of states that helps you to understand this.

Smith used this list to help Fred explore the problem with requirements.

Requirements is an example of an alpha. The Requirements alpha is typically manifested by a number of individual requirement items—for example, a set of features, user stories, or use cases (e.g., in Scrum the Requirements alpha is manifested by the product backlog, and the requirement items would be the user stories in the product backlog). In a more traditional setting the Requirements alpha could be manifested by a requirements document.

Fred's team had the habit of tracking the number of requirement items yet to be completed. Figure 2-2 shows the remaining requirement items for both the Enhancement requirements and the Value Added Services requirements.

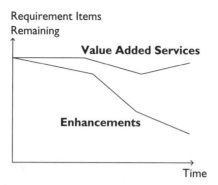

Figure 2-2 Requirement items remaining in Fred's team

What Is the Scope of the Requirements Alpha?

So, does this assume we always must assign a single state to *all* of the requirements for the endeavor? No, in real life different subsets of the total set of requirements will be of different levels of maturity. For example, Fred's team has two sets of requirements:

1. Enhancement requirements, which were progressing well

2. Value Added Services requirements, which were not converging

Therefore, which state is applicable is dependent on the scope you are currently looking at. For example, you could be considering the specific requirement items that you are going to address in the next iteration, or perhaps the subset of the requirements that are related to one of many new features. We will see this in Part II of the book when we discuss a small team doing agile development.

It is clear from Figure 2-2 that Enhancement requirements were progressing well, as the number of requirement items remaining decreases with time. Value Added Services requirements, however, were not progressing well; in fact, some of the completed requirement items in this group got invalidated, and Fred's team was frustrated.

2.3 ALPHAS HAVE STATES TO HELP A TEAM ACHIEVE PROGRESS

As we have shown, the kernel alphas can be used to explore the root causes of a challenge. The kernel can also help to overcome the challenge because each alpha has a series of states to guide a team to achieve progress and health.

Figure 2-3 shows the states for the Requirements alpha, which Smith used to explain to Fred and his team why his requirement items would not converge.

The Requirements alpha states are defined as follows.

- *Conceived:* The Requirements start in the Conceived state when the need for a new software system has been agreed on. The stakeholders can hold differing views on the overall meaning of the requirements. However, they all agree that there is a need for a new software system and a clear opportunity to be pursued.

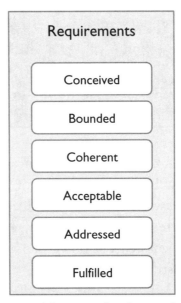

Figure 2-3 Requirements alpha states (read top to bottom)

- *Bounded:* The overall scope of the new system and the mechanisms for managing and accepting new or changed requirements are established. In the Bounded state there may still be inconsistencies among the individual requirement items. However, the stakeholders now have a shared understanding of the purpose of the new system and can tell whether or not a request qualifies as a valid requirement.

- *Coherent:* The essential characteristics of the new system are clearly defined. The requirement items continue to evolve as more is learned about the new system and its impact on its stakeholders and environment. No matter how much the requirement items change, it is essential that they stay within the bounds of the original concept and that they remain coherent at all times.

- *Acceptable:* The requirements define a system that will be acceptable to the stakeholders as, at least, an initial solution. The requirements may only describe a partial solution; however, the solution described is of sufficient value that the stakeholders would accept it for operational use.

- *Addressed:* Enough requirement items have been implemented for the new system to be worth releasing and using. In the Addressed state the number of requirement items that have been addressed is sufficient for the resultant system to provide clear value to the stakeholders. If the resultant system provides a complete solution, the requirements may advance immediately to the Fulfilled state.

- *Fulfilled:* Enough of the requirement items have been implemented for the stakeholders to agree that the resultant system fully satisfies the need for a new system, and that there are no outstanding requirement items preventing the system from being considered complete.

Smith explained the Requirements alpha states to Fred and asked him to identify the state of the Value Added Services requirements. Fred realized that his team did not have a clear idea of what Angela really wanted to achieve with the Value Added Services requirements, which were perhaps only at the Conceived state. Enhancement requirements, on the other hand, were progressing well and were already in the Acceptable state. Fred realized immediately that he would need to do something to get the Value Added Services requirements Bounded and Coherent before wasting further energy on development. Smith then worked with Fred to agree on what had to be done to achieve this. This meant working more closely with Angela and other stakeholders to help them clarify what they really wanted to achieve.

The Enhancement requirements, which were progressing well, were not stalled by this work. Fred's team members could continue with the good work they were doing.

Smith also helped Fred consider progress from the perspective of other alphas, such as Opportunity, Stakeholders, and Software System, to get them to a state representing a balanced progress in all dimensions of the development endeavor. The desired states were as follows.

- *Opportunity: Value Established*—The value of addressing the opportunity is understood. The impact of the solution on the stakeholders is understood.
- *Stakeholders: In Agreement*—The stakeholder representatives have been identified and are in agreement on minimal expectations to be met before the system can be deployed.
- *Requirements: Bounded*—The purpose and theme of the new system are clear.

- *Software System: Demonstrable*—An executable version of the system is available that demonstrates the architecture is fit for purpose and supports functional and nonfunctional testing.

2.4 THERE IS MORE TO THE KERNEL

In this chapter we did not look at the complete kernel. We only showed what Smith, Fred, and Angela needed to deal with in terms of their particular challenge. You can discuss and address many other challenges with the kernel, through other alphas.

Later in this book we will show how to use the kernel and how to scale the usage to different kinds of development, including small projects (in Part II and Part III) as well as big projects (in Part IV).

3

A 10,000-Foot View
of the Full Kernel

This chapter provides an overview of the kernel, including the key innovations of the kernel approach. We start by defining what a kernel is and what is new with the kernel approach. We then define the different kinds of elements in the kernel, which are

- The essential things to progress and evolve—the alphas
- The essential things to do—the activity spaces
- The essential capabilities needed—the competencies

You can view this chapter as an introduction to the proposal[1] submitted by the SEMAT community to the OMG.

Definition

A software engineering kernel is a lightweight set of concepts and definitions that captures the essence of effective, scalable software engineering in a practice-independent way. The kernel forms a common ground for describing and conducting software development.

---

1. The proposal submitted by SEMAT to the OMG can be found on the SEMAT website, www.semat.org.

While it is true that the kernel attempts to provide a concise list of words commonly found in software engineering, it is not a static dictionary that you read. The kernel is dynamic and actionable. By that we mean you can make the kernel come alive. You can use it in real life to run an endeavor (e.g., a project or sprint). It includes the essential elements always prevalent in every endeavor, such as Requirements, Software System, Team, and Work. These elements have states representing progress and health, so as the endeavor moves forward, these elements progress from state to state.

3.1 ORGANIZING THE KERNEL

The kernel is organized into three discrete *areas of concern,* each focusing on a specific dimension of software development. As shown in Figure 3-1, these are as follows.

- *Customer:* Software development always involves at least one customer for the software that it produces. The customer perspective must be integrated into the day-to-day work to ensure that an appropriate solution is developed. The customer area of concern contains everything to do with the actual use and exploitation of the software system to be produced.

- *Solution:* The goal of software development is to develop a working software system to solve some problem. The solution area of concern contains everything related to the specification and development of the software system.

- *Endeavor:* Software development is an endeavor of consequence that typically takes significant time and effort to complete, affects many different people, and involves a development team. The endeavor area of concern contains

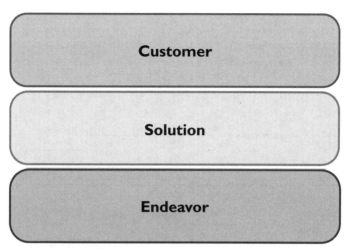

Figure 3-1 The three areas of concern

everything related to the development team and the way they do their work.

3.2 THE ESSENTIAL THINGS TO PROGRESS AND EVOLVE: THE ALPHAS

As we explained in Chapter 2, in every software development endeavor there are a number of things we always have, such as a team, and a number of things we always produce, such as a software system. These key elements are represented by the alphas of the kernel. For the sake of completeness we will now repeat some material presented earlier. All alphas in the kernel are shown in Figure 3-2.

- *Opportunity:* The set of circumstances that makes it appropriate to develop or change a software system. The opportunity articulates the reason for the creation of the new, or changed, software system. It represents the team's shared understanding of the stakeholder's needs, and helps shape

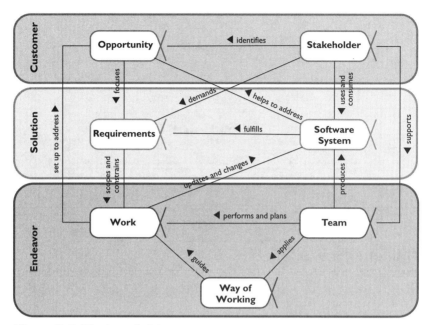

Figure 3-2 The kernel alphas

the requirements for the new software system by providing justification for its development.

- *Stakeholders:* The people, groups, or organizations that affect or are affected by a software system. The stakeholders provide the opportunity, and are the source of the requirements for the software system. They are involved throughout the software engineering endeavor to support the team and ensure that an acceptable software system is produced.

- *Requirements:* What the software system must do to address the opportunity and satisfy the stakeholders. It is important to discover what is needed from the software system, share this understanding among the stakeholders and the team members, and use it to drive the development and testing of the new system.

- *Software System:* A system, made up of software, hardware, and data, that provides its primary value by the execution of the software. The primary product of any software engineering endeavor, a software system can be part of a larger software, hardware, business, or social solution.

- *Team:* The group of people actively engaged in the development, maintenance, delivery, and support of a specific software system. The team plans and performs the work needed to create, update, and/or change the software system.

- *Work:* The activity involving mental or physical effort done in order to achieve a result. In the context of software development, work is everything the team does to work with a software system, matching the requirements and addressing the opportunity presented by the stakeholders. The work is guided by the practices that make up the team's way of working.

- *Way of Working:* The practices and tools used by a team to guide and support their work. This evolves with the team's understanding of their mission and their working environment. As the team proceeds they continually reflect on their way of working and adapt it as necessary to their current context.

Each alpha has a number of states that help you to understand the current status of your development endeavor and determine your next steps (see Figure 3-3).

Tied to each state is a set of criteria that concretely expresses what must be achieved in the state. These checklists are presented in two complementary formats: a brief summary and a full checklist. Table 3-1 shows the summary format and Table 3-2 the full checklist.

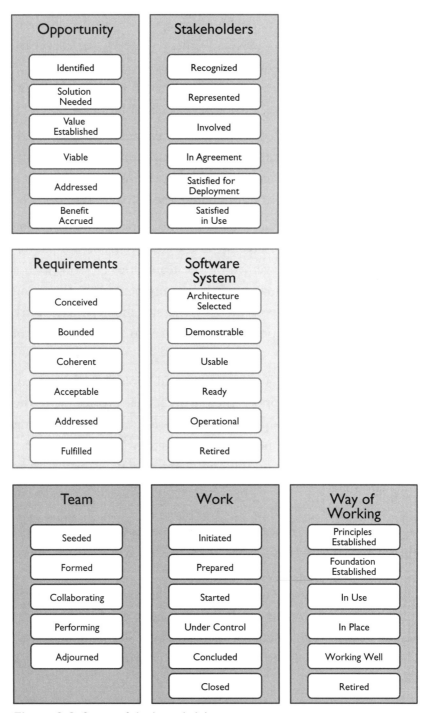

Figure 3-3 States of the kernel alphas

Table 3-1 Short-Form Checklist for the Requirements Alpha

State	Checklist
Conceived	• The need for a new system is clear. • Users are identified. • Initial sponsors are identified.
Bounded	• The purpose and extent of the system are agreed on. • Success criteria are clear. • Mechanisms for handling requirements are agreed on. • Constraints and assumptions are identified.
Coherent	• The big picture is clear and shared by all involved. • Important usage scenarios are explained. • Priorities are clear. • Conflicts are addressed. • Impact is understood.
Acceptable	• Requirements describe a solution acceptable to the stakeholders. • The rate of change to agreed-on requirements is low. • Value is clear.
Addressed	• Enough requirements are implemented for the system to be acceptable. • Stakeholders agree the system is worth making operational.
Fulfilled	• The system fully satisfies the requirements and the need. • There are no outstanding requirement items preventing completion.

Table 3-2 Full Checklist for Requirements

State	Checklist
Conceived	• The initial set of stakeholders agrees that a system is to be produced. • There is a clear opportunity for the new system to address. • The stakeholders that will use the new system are identified. • The stakeholders that will fund the initial work on the new system are identified.

continues

Table 3-2 Full Checklist for Requirements (*continued*)

State	Checklist
Bounded	• The stakeholders involved in developing the new system are identified. • The stakeholders agree on the purpose of the new system. • It is clear what success is for the new system. • The stakeholders have a shared understanding of the extent of the proposed solution. • The way the requirements will be described is agreed on. • The mechanisms for managing the requirements are in place. • The prioritization scheme is clear. • Constraints are identified and considered. • Assumptions are clearly stated.
Coherent	• The requirements are captured and shared with the team and the stakeholders. • The origin of the requirements is clear. • The rationale behind the requirements is clear. • Conflicting requirements are identified and attended to. • The requirements communicate the essential characteristics of the system to be delivered. • The most important usage scenarios for the system can be explained. • The priority of the requirements is clear. • The impact of implementing the requirements is understood. • The team understands what has to be delivered and agrees to deliver it.
Acceptable	• The stakeholders accept that the requirements describe an acceptable solution. • The rate of change to the agreed-on requirements is relatively low and under control. • The value provided by implementing the requirements is clear. • The parts of the opportunity satisfied by the requirements are clear.

Table 3-2 Full Checklist for Requirements (*continued*)

State	Checklist
Addressed	• Enough of the requirements are addressed for the resultant system to be acceptable to the stakeholders. • The stakeholders accept the requirements as accurately reflecting what the system does and does not do. • The set of requirement items implemented provides clear value to the stakeholders. • The system implementing the requirements is accepted by the stakeholders as worth making operational.
Fulfilled	• The stakeholders accept the requirements as accurately capturing what they require to fully satisfy the need for a new system. • There are no outstanding requirement items preventing the system from being accepted as fully satisfying the requirements. • The stakeholders accept the system as fully satisfying the requirements.

In the rest of this book, when we illustrate the use of the kernel we will use the short-form summary checklists. This is to keep things brief and succinct. The full checklists can be found in the Essence Specification.

What Is the Scope of the Alphas?

In the same way as for the Requirements alpha that we discussed in Chapter 2, the scope of an alpha and the state it is in are context-dependent. For a system that is developed in increments, potentially in parallel, what state is applicable will naturally depend on the increment you are considering. Similar things could be said for the other alphas, and it is always important to be clear on the current scope when considering the alpha states.

If you want to have a better understanding of the states, Part III includes a story of a development that goes through every alpha and every state.

3.3 THE ESSENTIAL THINGS TO DO: THE ACTIVITIES

In every software development endeavor you carry out a number of *activities*. Examples of activities include agreeing on a user story with a product owner, demonstrating the system to a customer representative, and estimating work. The kernel as such does not define any activities, but it does define a number of *activity spaces*. You can think of activity spaces as method-independent placeholders for specific activities that will be added later on top of the kernel.

The activity spaces of the kernel are shown in Figure 3-4 where they are denoted by dashed-arrowed pentagons and organized into the different areas of concern.

In addition to being placeholders for specific activities, the activity spaces represent the essential things that have to be done to develop good software. They provide general descriptions of the challenges a team faces when developing, maintaining, and supporting software systems, and the kinds of things the team

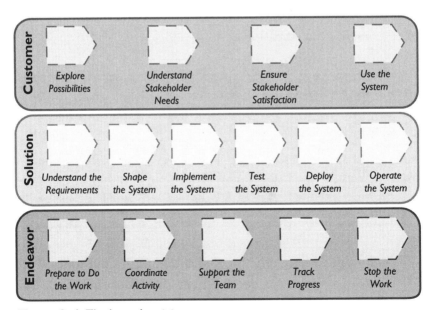

Figure 3-4 The kernel activity spaces

will do to meet them. Each activity space then can be extended with concrete activities that progress one or more of the kernel alphas.

In the top row of Figure 3-4 there are activity spaces to understand the opportunity, and to support and involve the stakeholders.

- *Explore Possibilities:* Explore the possibilities presented by a new or improved software system. This includes the analysis of the opportunity and the identification of the stakeholders.

- *Understand Stakeholder Needs:* Engage with the stakeholders to understand their needs and ensure that the right results are produced. This includes identifying and working with the stakeholder representatives to progress the opportunity.

- *Ensure Stakeholder Satisfaction:* Share the results of the development work with the stakeholders to gain their acceptance of the system produced and to verify that the opportunity has been addressed.

- *Use the System:* Use the system in a live environment to benefit the stakeholders.

In the middle row of Figure 3-4 there are activity spaces to develop an appropriate solution to exploit the opportunity and satisfy the stakeholders.

- *Understand the Requirements:* Establish a shared understanding of what the system must do.

- *Shape the System:* Shape the system to make it easy to develop, change, and maintain. This includes the overall design and architecture of the system.

- *Implement the System:* Build a system by implementing, testing, and integrating one or more system elements.

- *Test the System:* Verify that the system meets the stakeholders' requirements.

- *Deploy the System:* Take the tested system and make it available for use outside the development team.

- *Operate the System:* Support the use of the software system in the live environment.

In the bottom row of Figure 3-4 there are activity spaces to form a team and to progress the work in line with the agreed-on way of working.

- *Prepare to Do the Work:* Set up the team and its working environment. Understand and sign up for the work.

- *Coordinate Activity:* Coordinate and direct the team's work. This includes all ongoing planning and replanning of the work.

- *Support the Team:* Help the team members to help themselves, collaborate, and improve their way of working.

- *Track Progress:* Measure and assess the progress made by the team.

- *Stop the Work:* Shut down the work and hand over the team's responsibilities.

To make Figure 3-4 easy to read, the activity spaces are shown in a sequence from left to right in each row. The sequence indicates the order in which things are finished and not the order in which they are started. For example, you can start shaping the system before you have finished understanding the requirements, but you can't be sure you have finished shaping the system until you have finished understanding the requirements.

3.4 COMPETENCIES

To participate in a software endeavor you need to have competency in different areas. You need competency relevant to the specific tasks you are working on, but you also need other competencies to understand what your teammates are working on.

Competencies are defined in the kernel and can be thought of as generic containers for specific skills. Specific skills—for example, Java programming are not part of the kernel because such skills are not essential on *all* software engineering endeavors. But competency is always required, and it will be up to the individual teams to identify the specific skills needed for their particular software endeavors.

A common problem of software endeavors is not being aware of the gap between the competency that is needed and the competency that is available. The kernel approach will raise the visibility of this gap.

At the time of this writing (August 2012) the SEMAT group has not yet decided on a set of specific competencies to be part of the kernel. But to illustrate the concept, Figure 3-5 presents some possible competencies that may or may not become part of the kernel as the work in SEMAT continues.

The example competencies in Figure 3-5 are as follows.

- **Stakeholder Representation:** This competency encapsulates the ability to gather, communicate, and balance the needs of other stakeholders, and accurately represent their views.

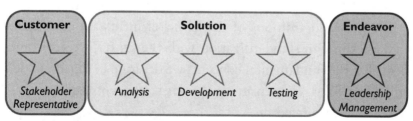

Figure 3-5 Example of competencies

- **Analysis:** This competency encapsulates the ability to understand opportunities and their related stakeholder needs, and to transform them into an agreed upon and consistent set of requirements.

- **Development:** This competency encapsulates the ability to design and program effective software systems following the standards and norms agreed upon by the team.

- **Testing:** This competency encapsulates the ability to test a system, verifying that it is usable and that it meets the requirements.

- **Leadership:** This competency enables a person to inspire and motivate a group of people to achieve a successful conclusion to their work and to meet their objectives.

- **Management:** This competency encapsulates the ability to coordinate, plan, and track the work done by a team.

3.5 FINDING OUT MORE ABOUT THE KERNEL

In this chapter we presented a snapshot of the kernel. The work on the kernel is still ongoing within SEMAT (www.semat.org). At the time of this writing (August 2012), this group has identified a set of alphas and a set of activity spaces, but is still working on competencies. Activity spaces and competencies are not the focus of this book, so we will not describe them further. We mention them in this chapter just to give you an overview of the elements of the full kernel.

Finding the right elements of the kernel is crucial. They must be universally acceptable, significant, relevant, and guided by the notion that "You have achieved perfection not when there is nothing left to add, but when there is nothing left to take away."[2]

Even if the definitions of the kernel elements are adjusted as they go through standardization with the OMG, we are confident that the fundamental concepts we describe in this book will still apply. SEMAT is ensuring that these concepts and elements will be widely agreed on.

---

2. Antoine de Saint-Exupéry

4

The Kernel Alphas Made Tangible with Cards

The kernel captures the essence of software engineering—the essential concepts to run software endeavors, to solve challenges, and to communicate and collaborate effectively. But how do you learn the kernel?

One way is through the use of cards. Cards have proven to be a lightweight and practical way not only to remember the kernel, but also to use it in practice in a team.

Cards make the elements of the kernel—particularly alphas, which are the emphasis of this book—easy to digest and use. For this reason, we present the alphas in two ways: through alpha definition cards and alpha state cards. We will continue with the discussion involving Smith, Fred, and Angela to demonstrate the usefulness of these two kinds of cards.

4.1 USING CARDS AS AIDS TO ADDRESS A SPECIFIC CHALLENGE: AN EXAMPLE

Recall that in Sections 1.3.1 and 2.2 Smith had to help Fred solve his challenge with requirements. When talking with Fred, Smith used words such as *opportunity, requirements, stakeholders,* and *software system.* These words were unfamiliar to Fred, and Smith had to explain them.

Smith first showed a Requirements *alpha definition card* (about the size of a 5 × 3-inch index card), which lists the essential qualities of good requirements and the Requirements alpha's state progression (see Figure 4-1). Smith showed this card because Fred had requirements problems to begin with. Gradually, Smith put all the related alpha definition cards on the table as he explored the challenge with Fred. Through the alpha definition cards, Fred could explore the different dimensions of his situation.

As the discussion proceeded, Smith had to clarify the meaning of each alpha state. So he laid out another set of cards, the *alpha state cards,* each about the size of a business card. Each state card has the name of its alpha, the name of its state, and a list of criteria for achieving that state. As before, Smith started with the Requirements alpha and placed the state cards on the table in front of Fred (see Figure 4-2). The numbers at the bottom of each state card indicate the order of the state and the total number of states for that alpha.

Smith pointed to the Conceived state card and told Fred, "This is where you are, and you are trying to create the finished product. Of course, it will seem that you are working on a set of random requests." Smith then pointed to the Bounded state and said, "This is where you need to be to understand if a particular requirement is at all relevant or not. Only then can you start implementing the most important requirements." Finally,

Opportunity

The set of circumstances that makes it appropriate to develop or change a software system

- A good opportunity is identified addressing the need for a software-based solution
- A good opportunity has established value
- A good opportunity has a software-based solution that can be produced quickly and cheaply
- A good opportunity creates a tangible benefit

- Identified
- Solution Needed
- Value Established
- Viable
- Addressed
- Benefit Accrued

Stakeholders

The people, groups, or organizations who affect or are affected by a software system

- Healthy stakeholders represent groups or organizations affected by the software system
- Healthy stakeholder representatives carry out their agreed-on responsibilities
- Healthy stakeholder representatives cooperate to reach agreement
- Healthy stakeholders are satisfied with the use of the software system

- Recognized
- Represented
- Involved
- In Agreement
- Satisfied for Deployment
- Satisfied in Use

Requirements

What the software system must do to address the opportunity and satisfy the stakeholders

- Good Requirements meet real needs
- Good Requirements have clear scope
- Good Requirements are coherent and well organized
- Good Requirements help drive development

- Conceived
- Bounded
- Coherent
- Acceptable
- Addressed
- Fulfilled

Software System

A system made up of software, hardware, and data that provides its primary value by the execution of the software

- Good Software System meets requirements
- Good Software System has appropriate architecture
- Good Software System is maintainable, extensible, and testable
- Good Software System has low support cost

- Architecture Selected
- Demonstrable
- Usable
- Ready
- Operational
- Retired

Figure 4-1 Alpha definition cards that Smith used to explore the problem

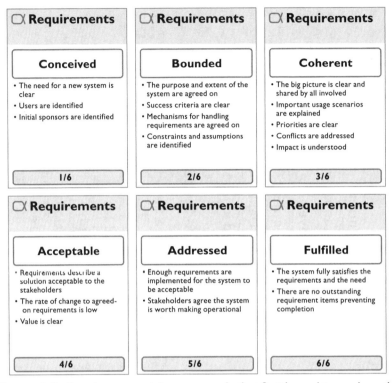

Figure 4-2 Requirements alpha state cards that Smith used to explore the situation

Smith pointed to the Acceptable state and continued, "This is where you want to be to be sure that you have understood all the requirements that are needed for the system to be acceptable." Smith then moved the Addressed and Fulfilled state cards away as they were not relevant to their discussion. Fred shifted each state card slightly as an indication that he had finished reading it.

Fred and Angela then ran a series of workshops to discuss different subsets of the requirements, and Smith was invited to sit in to observe and facilitate. To kick off the workshops, Smith put the target state cards on the whiteboard. This acted as a reminder of the objectives of the workshop. As an example, during the Understand Requirements workshop for the Value Added Services, Smith put the Requirements alpha definition card and the Conceived, Bounded, and Coherent state cards on the whiteboard.

When discussions strayed, Smith would point toward the cards. At the end of each session, Fred and Angela would review to determine if they had achieved the states based on the listed criteria.

By observing what Smith was pointing at on the cards, both Fred and Angela were able to articulate why it was difficult to agree on the requirements, how this was impacting their work, and how to address the issue. By using the kernel, and reinforcing it with the cards, the whole team was soon using the same vocabulary.

The cards are just one of the many possible techniques to help developers remember the kernel and apply it. However, our experience is that most teams need some mechanism to keep the states of the alphas and their checklists visible during their daily activities. When we say the kernel is actionable, we mean it isn't just a description of what someone would like the team to do. It represents what the team actually does and includes the team's actual progress and health. As developers go about their daily work, the results of what they do are reflected in the states of the kernel elements. This helps everyone on the team, regardless of experience, to have a shared understanding of where the team is and where it is going.

4.2 MAKING THE KERNEL COME ALIVE

The alpha definition cards and alpha state cards are lightweight. Alpha definition cards are the size of 5 × 3-inch index cards and summarize what an alpha is about. Alpha state cards are the size of business cards. This is fundamentally different from traditional methods described in thick books and heavyweight manuals. Having said this, more elaborate descriptions still have value for team members who want to go deeper.

Cards are tangible. You can easily move cards around during discussions. The tangible nature of the cards is very important. It makes the kernel concrete and come alive. We have worked with teams where each member carries a stack of alpha state cards with them. Other teams keep the alphas and their states visible as reminder sheets tacked up in their team area.

We have worked with teams who print enlarged state cards, put the cards on their whiteboard, and use them as part of their daily stand-up meetings. This gets team members to view alpha state criteria on a daily basis. They use these criteria to determine if they have reached a particular state and what else they need to do to reach that state. Putting up the criteria for everyone on the team to see helps to build a common understanding quickly. This is in contrast to more traditional approaches where such information is kept in large documents, which seldom are referenced, at least during daily meetings. How to use cards will be discussed in more detail later in the book.

5

Providing More Details to the Kernel through Practices

The kernel captures the common ground that underlies all software engineering. As a software professional, the kernel helps you to understand the challenges you face; however, it does not tell you how to address these challenges. In simple cases, or when your team members are experienced, you can easily figure out what needs to be done. However, in more complex situations, you are likely to need more guidance.

As we saw in Chapters 1 and 2, Smith and the team used the kernel as a thinking aid to analyze and understand their problems. In this chapter we will see how they created a simple requirements elicitation practice to improve their way of working. This practice provides the details for the team members to address their particular challenges. With a good understanding of this practice, the team is able to address similar challenges in the future.

Definition

A practice is a repeatable approach to doing something with a specific purpose in mind.

Now, a team usually faces several challenges. This means they may need several practices. The composition of these practices is what we call a *method*.

5.1 MAKING A PRACTICE EXPLICIT

In Chapter 1 we saw how Smith helped Fred and Angela overcome their problem with requirements. This is an example of applying a practice: a requirements elicitation practice. Smith had what he needed in his head, and the practice was tacit—it was only manifested in the conversations among Smith, Fred, and Angela. When you scale up and have multiple teams, possibly with similar challenges, it is probably a good idea to describe practices explicitly to avoid someone like Smith becoming a bottleneck. The kernel provides a lightweight language and approach to capture practices, focusing on what the team produces and does.

Now, in this particular case, what Smith recommended to Fred and Angela did not change what they produced, that is, in what form requirements were captured—for example, by replacing a traditional requirements document with user stories. Rather, Smith's recommendation was about what they must do to come to an agreement on requirements, through clarifying the opportunity by involving stakeholders.

Smith's practice for requirements collaboration involves several activities, making the activity spaces Explore Possibilities, Understand the Requirements, and Understand Stakeholder Needs more explicit. A summary of the resultant practices is shown in Figure 5-1.

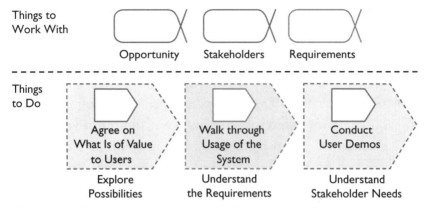

Figure 5-1 Example of a requirements elicitation practice

The activities are as follows.

- *Agree on what is of value to users.* Review the success criteria for the system, what its differentiators are, and what the values are that the system needs to deliver to its intended users.

- *Walk through usage of the system.* Walk through the use of the system step by step, and discuss the value the system brings to the user at each step. Discuss and agree on what information users are interested in seeing, and what the user is interested in doing.

- *Conduct user demos.* Conduct demos that walk through usage of the system from the user's point of view as a confirmation of the aforementioned walkthrough.

The team conducts these activities to progress the Requirements, Stakeholders, and Opportunity.

5.2 HOW EXPLICIT SHOULD PRACTICES BE?

Practice descriptions provide additional guidance on top of the kernel in terms of how to do things. They can also describe the work products to be developed. How explicit a practice should be, that is, how detailed the descriptions should be, depends on two factors.

- *Capability:* Capabilities refers to a person's ability to, based on the knowledge they already have, figure things out for themselves. Team members with high skill and capability need only a few reminders and examples to get going. Others may need training and coaching to learn how to apply a practice effectively.

- *Background:* If the team has worked together using a practice in the past or has gone through the same training, they have a shared background. In this case, practices can be tacit. On the other hand, if team members have been using different practices—for example, some have been using traditional requirements specifications while others have been using user stories—they have different backgrounds. In this case, practices should be described to avoid miscommunication.

Figure 5-2 summarizes how these two factors interact and influence the form your practices should take.

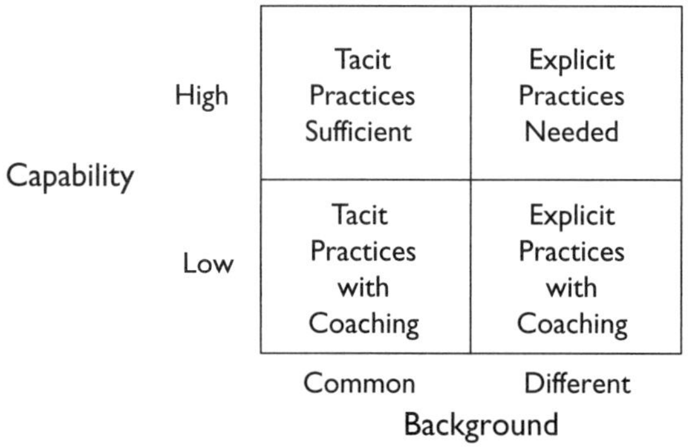

		Common	Different
Capability	High	Tacit Practices Sufficient	Explicit Practices Needed
	Low	Tacit Practices with Coaching	Explicit Practices with Coaching
		Background	

Figure 5-2 How explicit practices should be depends on capability and background

In the case of Fred's requirements challenges, the situation was that Fred and Angela had different backgrounds and they didn't know that much about requirements collaboration techniques. Thus, they needed explicit practices and some coaching, which was what Smith provided.

5.3 BUILDING METHODS FROM PRACTICES

As mentioned earlier, a team usually faces a number of challenges and would need the guidance of several practices. Starting with the kernel a team selects a number of practices and tools to make up its way of working. The set of practices that they select for their way of working is their method (see Figure 5-3). The term *method* is also used to describe a predefined set of practices that provide a standard, reusable way of working for use within a specific context. If a suitable method is available, the team can use this as a starting point instead of building their method from scratch.

Even if there are many different methods (every team, or at the least, every organization, has one), they are not as different as it may seem. Examples of common practices are user stories, test-driven development, and backlog-driven development.

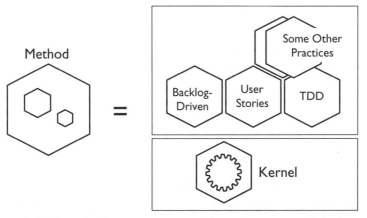

Figure 5-3 A method is a composition of practices on top of the kernel

The kernel provides a common ground that is independent of any particular practice, meaning that any method can be seen as a set of practices on top of the kernel. Some practices may be described while some may be kept tacit.

> ### How Much Does a Developer Need to Know about Methods?
>
> At this point, you may be asking yourself whether you really need to care about all of this method theory. Remember, a method is a description of the team's way of working and it provides help and guidance to the team as they perform their task. What the kernel does is help you structure what you do in a way that supports incremental evolution. In other words, it puts you in control of the way you work and provides the tools to change it.

5.4 LEARNING METHODS AND PRACTICES

The kernel helps you to learn different methods and practices.

- *Learning and training based on a common ground:* When learning a new practice or method, perhaps feature-driven development, use cases, or user stories, it is sometimes difficult to see how it will fit with your current way of working. By basing the practices on a common ground, you can easily relate new practices to what you already have. You learn the kernel once and then you just focus on what is different with each new practice.

- *Learning and training focused on the essentials:* The essentials are usually just a small fraction of what an expert knows about a subject, but if well selected they are enough to get started. Learning the essentials enables anyone to participate in conversations about your work without having all the details. It helps to grow T-shaped[1] people, who have

---

1. http://en.wikipedia.org/wiki/T-shaped_skills

expertise in a particular field, but also broad knowledge across other fields. Such people are what the industry needs as work becomes more multidisciplinary. Once you have learned the essentials, it is relatively straightforward to find out more by yourself from different sources.

The idea of describing practices on top of the kernel is a key theme of this book. Actually, we demonstrated this idea in Smith's story in the earlier chapters. In the next part of the book we will go into a bit more detail to see what really went on under the surface. A fuller discussion of how practices are formed on top of the kernel is found in Part IV.

6

What the Kernel Can Do for You

As a software professional, you want to create great software quickly. You want to deal flexibly with challenges as they appear. As you advance in your career, you want to take on new, larger challenges, learn new domains and technologies, and apply new practices and methods (see Figure 6-1).

To do this, you need to always be learning, and the way you and your team works must always be evolving. This learning and evolving must come naturally and should build on what you already know and do.

Figure 6-1 What software professionals do

Let's discuss how the kernel can help.

- *Develop great software:* The kernel helps you address typical challenges, as we have demonstrated earlier in the book with the stories of Fred, Angela, and Smith. We have seen how the kernel alphas help you to see progress and recognize health in what you do. We have seen how the kernel can improve communication in a team.

- *Grow:* The kernel helps you grow by providing a firm foundation for your experiences and your team's way of working. Not only is the kernel useful for small software endeavors involving small teams, but you can also use it in endeavors involving hundreds of people.

- *Learn:* When you join a new team, you want to learn the team's way of working. When you decide to use a new technique in your team, you need to get everyone up to speed using it. The kernel improves communication, allowing for quick learning.

- *Evolve:* Evolving means you can incrementally improve your way of working. It means you can change without throwing away more than what needs to be changed.

We will now look into this in more detail.

6.1 DEVELOPING GREAT SOFTWARE

Traditional methods are static; they may help you appreciate new ideas, but they don't help you while you actually do your job. Their descriptions are often heavyweight and do not match what you see or do in practice. Two things set the kernel approach apart from the traditional way of describing methods.

- **The kernel has focus on progress and health.** The alphas are the key to this. The alphas are not just helpful to describe your method; they also guide you in achieving progress and health while you actually use the method. Each alpha has a series of states and each state has a set of checkpoints, which must be achieved before the state is reached. Hence, as your software endeavor proceeds, you will also proceed through the state of the alphas. Thus, you can, at every moment of a software endeavor, assess which states have been achieved, thereby understanding progress and health.

- **The kernel is actionable.** In addition to understanding where you are, the states of the alphas guide you where to go next. The checklists for each state provide the first level of guidance for how to achieve a state. In addition to that, activity spaces and activities are tied to the state progressions and provide additional guidance on how to achieve future states.

What Is Different with the Kernel Approach When It Comes to Measurement?

The software community has tried to measure progress and health for 40 years. So, what is different with the kernel approach when it comes to measurement? The kernel is based on a broad experience base and contains the essentials that can help you measure software progress and health. This help is expressed as simple checklists associated with each state of the kernel alphas.

For example, developers who use the kernel know that to determine whether they have achieved the Bounded state for requirements, they must ask themselves the following questions.

- Is it clear what success means for this new system?
- Have we identified all the stakeholders and do they have a shared understanding of the proposed solution?
- Has the way the requirements will be described been agreed on?
- Is the prioritization scheme clear?
- Are the assumptions and constraints clear?

There is no magic with these questions. But the power comes from having a widely agreed-on set of questions to determine progress and health. Use of the kernel will thereby make it easier to assess and communicate progress with both your teammates and your stakeholders.

6.2 GROWING

The kernel provides the common ground for all software professionals to share. By learning the kernel you establish a firm foundation for your own personal growth. Understanding the kernel will allow you to put your experiences into context, understand your contribution to the team, and plan your personal development by selecting new areas to explore or complementary practices to learn.

The broad experience of those involved in developing the kernel guarantees that the kernel is applicable in many different situations in many different domains. But this doesn't mean it solves all possible problems.

This is why the kernel is extensible. You can scale to your unique needs. There are three different dimensions of scaling.

- *Zooming in:* This is about providing additional guidance beyond what the kernel provides when your team members have different backgrounds or different levels of competencies. This additional guidance comes in the form of practices.

- *Reaching out:* This is about dealing with different kinds of development (e.g., in-house, offshore, bespoke, products, etc.). Each has different kinds of challenges and hence needs different methods comprising different practices.

- *Scaling up:* This is about dealing with situations involving a large number of requirements, more than one system, a large number of people, and so on.

How you scale in these three different dimensions is described in Part IV.

6.3 LEARNING

The usual ways for people to learn include reading papers and books, taking courses, and learning on the job from colleagues. This can get very confusing for the reader as the lack of any common ground between the sources can lead to people saying the same thing in different ways and different things in the same way.

Authors and readers would all benefit from adopting the kernel-based approach for the following reasons.

- The papers, courses, articles, and so on could all share the common ground, making them easier to understand and relate to one another.
- Authors could focus on their innovations without the need to cover everything related to developing software.

The best way to learn, though, is by practicing. The kernel-based approach to running a software endeavor, and building your way of working, encourages you to practice and learn by doing.

It will also help you to change teams and positions in an organization by giving you the thinking tools needed to relate your previous experiences to your new situation.

6.4 EVOLVING

Ideally, changes to your way of working are evolutionary and not revolutionary. You cannot casually throw away your existing way of working when a new method appears. You may have developed products with it that should live for many years to come.

Further, it is unlikely that all is bad; there are typically things in your existing way of working that you want to keep.

To make evolutionary changes to your way of working, you need to identify the parts of your way of working to replace and the parts to keep. For example, if a team wants to move from a traditional waterfall development method to an iterative development method, does that mean everything needs to change? Or can the team keep its way of capturing requirements, planning, designing, testing, its team organization, and so on?

A Key Difference with the Kernel Approach

Evolving is a key difference with the kernel approach. While it is true that in some occasions a team may need a more revolutionary reset of their way of working, it is far more common that a team's way of working is fundamentally working fine and is best improved one step at a time.

Today most methods are described and taught in a way that makes it difficult to change things one at a time. The kernel approach, on the other hand, supports evolutionary change in a way that allows teams to evolve their way of working as they go. Hence, the kernel is well aligned with lean concepts such as *Kaizen* and *Teams evolve practices.*

In Parts II and III of the book we will demonstrate how the kernel helps you to evolve your way of working incrementally. In Part II we will discuss simple evolutions in an intuitive way, and in Part III we will discuss the same ideas in a more structured way.

FURTHER READING

Jacobson, I., P.W. Ng, and I. Spence. 2007. "Enough of Processes: Let's Do Practices." *Journal of Object Technology* 6(6):41–67.

Jacobson, I., and I. Spence. "Why We Need a Theory for Software Engineering." *Dr. Dobb's Journal,* 2 October 2009.

Jacobson, I., B. Meyer, and R. Soley. "The SEMAT Initiative: A Call for Action." *Dr. Dobb's Journal,* 10 December 2009.

Jacobson, I. "Discover the Essence of Software Engineering." *CSI Communications,* July 2011.

Ng, P.W., and M. Magee. "Light Weight Application Lifecycle Management Using State-Cards." *Agile Journal,* 12 October 2010.

PART II

USING THE KERNEL TO RUN AN ITERATION

In this part of the book we will tell a story about how a small team uses the kernel to run an iteration—how they develop a small but stable increment of their system in a short, two- to four-week timebox.

The story we will tell is simpler than it would have been in real life as the purpose is to show how the kernel is used rather than being a complete account of everything that is done in an iteration.

7

Running Iterations with the Kernel: Plan-Do-Check-Adapt

The main character in our story is Smith. He had to develop a mobile application to browse a social network (e.g., Facebook, Google+) offline. The idea for this application came from Angela, Smith's customer representative from the marketing department. The application was to cache contents from the user's social network in the user's mobile device, thereby making it possible, as an example, to look at photos without a network connection.

We will look at how Smith and the team perform their development iteratively by walking through one of their iterations.

7.I TERMINOLOGY USED

The subject of this book is how the kernel can help software professionals in everyday situations. To keep it short we have left out many things that are already well known regarding agile planning and execution. However, to be clear the following terminology is used throughout the book when we discuss iterative working.

- *Iteration:* An iteration is a timebox intended to work with a stable increment of a software system. The length of an iteration is typically two to four weeks and can involve all kinds of activities, from requirements elicitation to the deployment of the resultant software system. The software system, and the team's understanding of it, is typically grown over a number of iterations.

- *Iteration objective:* As well as having the objective to work with the next stable increment of the software system, you may want to define additional objectives to be achieved in the iteration. These can include getting some key risk under control, demonstrating completely new functionality, establishing a new way of working, and so on. The iteration objectives can often be tied to progressing one or more of the kernel alpha states.

- *Iteration backlog:* When the team agrees on what is to be done in the iteration, they add the objectives to the iteration backlog. The iteration backlog can then be refined with more detail by adding the tasks necessary to achieve the objectives.

- *Task:* A task is a portion of work that can be clearly identified, isolated, and then accepted by one or more team members for completion. Each iteration objective is broken down into one or more tasks for the team to manage in the iteration backlog.

7.2 PLAN-DO-CHECK-ADAPT

Developing your software iteratively is like taking a journey in your car. You need to know where you are, where you are heading, how much fuel you have, and how much farther you have to go before reaching your destination. You adapt to the road

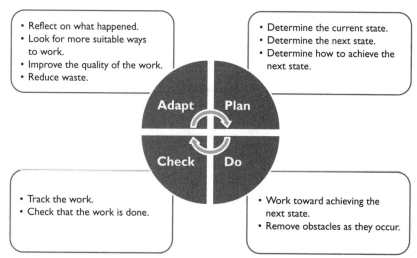

Figure 7-1 Plan-Do-Check-Adapt cycle

We have modified Deming's PDCA cycle by replacing Act with Adapt, as this is more descriptive of the intent.

conditions, traffic, and weather as you drive. You are continually planning, doing, checking, and adapting (see Figure 7-1). This is how Smith and his team ran their iterations.

- *Plan:* First, Smith's team determined the current state of the whole endeavor by determining the current state of each alpha. Then, based on this, they defined what alphas and states to progress in the coming iteration. They then planned how to achieve the target states by identifying tasks to be completed to achieve these states. This enabled them to tie in the detailed day-to-day work of the team with the progress of the endeavor as a whole. If the effort to complete the tasks exceeds that available in the iteration, then it will take more than a single iteration to achieve the objectives and the target states.

- *Do:* With each iteration, Smith's team worked on the identified tasks to progress the endeavor as a whole toward the target states. This involved writing code, testing, setting up environments, discussing requirements, writing documentation, and so on.

- *Check:* Smith's team tracked the objectives and tasks to make sure they were completing what they had planned (or they replanned as required) and that they followed their agreed-on way of working.

- *Adapt:* Smith's team reviewed their way of working, identified impediments, and found better or more suitable ways of doing things. This often resulted in changes to their plans and their way of working.

7.3 SETTING THE SCENE

The company had very little in the way of formal processes. It relied on having skilled and creative individuals. This had worked well in the past for experienced teams. But the company was growing and there were many new hires. The new hires, mostly fresh out of university, had good technical skills—for example, in programming languages—but were less equipped in other aspects of software development—for example, working with stakeholders to gain agreement on requirements.

When starting out, Smith's team had only two developers, Tom and himself. Both were familiar with the kernel. They were later joined by two other developers, Dick and Harriet, who were new to the job and had no previous knowledge of the kernel.

Success to Smith meant more than functionality, schedule, and quality. It also meant growing his new team members' competence in the different areas of the kernel.

At the outset the team members had different perspectives on their responsibilities, which we illustrate with the help of the kernel (see Figure 7-2).

	Angela	Dave	Smith	Tom	Dick and Harriet
Opportunity	✔	✔	✔		
Stakeholder	✔	✔			
Requirements	✔	✔	✔	✔	✔
Software System	✔	✔	✔	✔	✔
Work		✔	✔	✔	
Team			✔	✔	
Way of Working			✔	✔	✔

Figure 7-2 Views of the kernel of different participants

- *Angela, the customer representative:* Her main responsibility was to ensure the software system addressed the opportunity through continuous involvement of stakeholders (her department colleagues, and department head).

- *Dave, the department manager:* His primary concern was to make sure something of value was delivered on time and within budget.

- *Smith, the senior member of the development team:* He was the only developer with full knowledge of the company, its products, and its way of working.

- *Tom, an experienced developer Smith had worked with before:* He knew the kernel but had little knowledge of the best way to identify opportunities or work with the stakeholders.

- *Dick and Harriet, new developers:* They loved to code and to write good software. However, they were not up to speed on the company's way of working.

Smith's challenge was not just to produce a new software system, but also to build an effective software development team.

7.4 THE FOCUS FOR THE NEXT FEW CHAPTERS

Because the kernel alphas are universal, even small, noncomplex endeavors, such as Smith's, work with all seven of them. But for this specific story, to simplify things we just look at three alphas (see Figure 7-3).

As mentioned before, the team had agreed to do the work in iterations, where each iteration would result in a limited but stable version of the software system. To manage the work for the system, the team used their iteration backlog where they captured the iteration objectives and broke these down into more detailed tasks.

In each iteration the team always did the following:

1. Addressed more of the requirements

2. Produced a new increment of the software system

3. Applied and improved their way of working

They also checked the progress and health of all the alphas, including the Opportunity, Stakeholders, Work, and Team, but

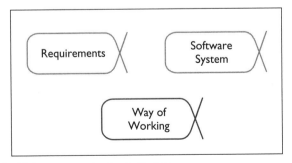

Figure 7-3 Alphas to emphasize in Smith's team

to keep things simple we will just focus on Requirements, Software System, and Way of Working.

In the rest of this part of the book, we will look at each element of the Plan-Do-Check-Adapt cycle in turn, and show how Smith's team used the kernel to help develop good software and improve their way of working.

8
Planning an Iteration

The art of planning an iteration is in deciding which of the many things the team has to do should be done in this iteration—the next two to four weeks. Every iteration will produce working software, but there are other things the team needs to think about. They need to make sure they develop the right software in the best way they can. The kernel helps the team reason about the current development context, and what to emphasize next, to make sure a good balance is achieved across the different dimensions of software development.

You can think of planning an iteration as follows.

1. *Determine where you are.* Work out the current state of the endeavor.

2. *Determine where to go.* Decide what to emphasize next, and what the objectives of the next iteration will be.

3. *Determine how to get there.* Agree on the tasks the team needs to do to achieve the objectives.

In our story, because of the way the team chose to run their iterations, the iteration objectives were put into the team's iteration backlog and broken down into more detailed tasks. In this way the iteration backlog served as the team's to-do list. We will now look at how Smith and his team used the alphas to guide the planning and execution of an iteration.

8.1 PLANNING GUIDED BY ALPHA STATES

When you plan an iteration the alphas can help you understand where you are and where to go next. By aligning the objectives they set for each iteration, Smith's team made sure they progressed in a balanced and cohesive way. This relationship between the alphas, and the objectives and tasks in the iteration backlog, is illustrated in Figure 8-1.

8.1.1 Determine Where You Are

When preparing for an iteration, the first step is to understand where you are. This involves, among other things, understanding details relating to technology, risks, quality, and stakeholder needs. But it is also important to have a shared understanding of where you are with the software endeavor as a whole, and this is where the kernel can help.

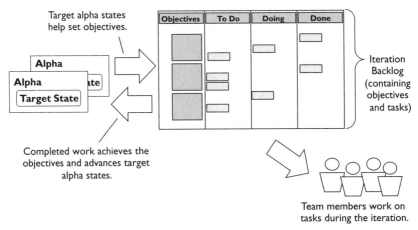

Figure 8-1 Working from the tasks and objectives in an iteration backlog

There are a number of ways you can use the kernel to do this. If you are using alpha state cards, as discussed in Part I, you can do this as follows.

- **Walkthrough:** This is a simple approach using one set of cards.

  1. Lay out the cards for each alpha in a row on a table with the first state on the left and the final state on the right.

  2. Walk through each state and ask your team if you have achieved that state.

  3. If the state is achieved, move that state card to the left. Continue with the next state card until you get to the state that your team has not yet achieved.

  4. Move this state card and the rest of the pending state cards to the right.

- **Poker:** Another approach that sometimes works better is poker.

  1. Each member is given a deck of state cards.

  2. For each alpha, each member selects the state card that he or she thinks best represents the current state of the software development endeavor.

  3. All members put their selected state card face down on the table.

  4. When all are ready, they turn the state card face up.

  5. If all members have selected the same state card, then there is consensus.

  6. If the selected state cards are different, it is likely there are different interpretations of the checklists for the states. The team can then discuss the checklists for the state to reach an agreement.

Using state cards is not required to use the kernel, but they are a useful tool to get the team members to talk, and to discuss what state the endeavor is in and what state they need to focus on next.

Once you have determined the current state of the endeavor, you can start discussing what the next set of states to be achieved should be.

8.1.2 Determine Where to Go

Identifying a set of desired alpha states guides the team in determining what to emphasize in an iteration. In fact, the iteration objective can be described as reaching a set of target alpha states.

Once the team has determined the current state of their alphas ,it is fairly easy to select which of the next states they should target in their next iteration. The target states make well-formed objectives as their checklists provide clearly defined completion criteria.

Selecting the target states can easily be done as an extension to the walkthrough and poker techniques described in the preceding section.

8.1.3 Determine How to Get There

After identifying a candidate set of objectives for the iteration, the team has to decide how they will address them and whether or not they can achieve them in the iteration timebox. Typically this is done by identifying one or more tasks to be completed to achieve the objective.

Again the alpha states help the team with the checklist for each state providing hints as to what tasks they will need to do to achieve the objective. In this part of the book we are just considering a small software endeavor. Later in the book we will discuss how you identify tasks and measure progress on more complex efforts.

8.2 DETERMINING THE CURRENT STATE IN OUR STORY

Smith and his team were six weeks into development. They had provided an early demonstration of the system to their stakeholders. Angela and the other stakeholders were pleased with what they saw, and they gave valuable feedback. However, the system was not yet usable by end users.

Smith started the iteration planning session with a walk-through to determine the current state. Figure 8-2 shows the states they had achieved on the left, and the states not yet achieved on the right.

Table 8-1 shows the current states for the alphas and describes how the team in our story achieved them.

8.3 DETERMINING THE NEXT STATE IN OUR STORY

Once the team had agreed on the current alpha states, the team discussed what the next desired "target" states were to guide its planning. The team agreed to use the immediate next alpha states to help establish the objectives of the next iteration. These are shown in Figure 8-3.

In most cases, the name of the alpha state itself provides sufficient information to understand the state. But if needed, team members can find out more by reading the alpha state checklist. By going through the states one by one for each alpha, a team quickly gets familiar with what is required to achieve each state. In this way the team learns about the kernel alphas at the same time as they determine their current state of development and their next target states.

8.4 DETERMINING HOW TO ACHIEVE THE NEXT STATES IN OUR STORY

Smith and his team looked at the next target states and agreed that some prioritization was needed. In this case, they needed

Table 8-1 How the Team Achieved the Current State of Development

Current State	How It Was Achieved
◑ Requirements **Acceptable** • Requirements describe a solution acceptable to the stakeholders • The rate of change to agreed-on requirements is low • Value is clear 4/6	Smith's team had demonstrated an early version of the application based on an initial set of requirements. After the demonstration, the stakeholders agreed that the understanding of the requirements was acceptable. The agreed-on requirement items were online and offline browsing of the social network, and making posts offline. However, these requirement items were only partially implemented at the time of the demonstration. According to the state definition, our team has achieved the Requirements: Acceptable state.
◑ Software System **Demonstrable** • Key architecture characteristics demonstrated • Relevant stakeholders agree architecture is appropriate • Critical interface and system configurations exercised 2/6	Early during development, Smith's team had identified the critical technical issues for the software system and outlined the architecture. This had allowed them to achieve the Software System: Architecture Selected state. Moreover, Smith's team had demonstrated an early version of the system to their stakeholders. This means that Smith's team had achieved the Software System: Demonstrable state. However, since Smith's team had not completed enough functionality to allow users to employ the system on their own, Smith's team had not yet achieved the Software System: Usable state.
◑ Way of Working **In Place** • All members of team are using way of working • All members have access to practices and tools to do their work • Whole team involved in inspection and adaptation of way of working 4/6	The two new members, Dick and Harriet, who had just come on board were not fully productive yet. In particular, they seemed to have trouble with the approach to automated testing, which the team agreed was important to maintain high quality during development. They had difficulty identifying good test cases and writing good test code. As such, the team agreed that the Way of Working is currently in the In Place state. But they had not yet achieved the Working Well state.

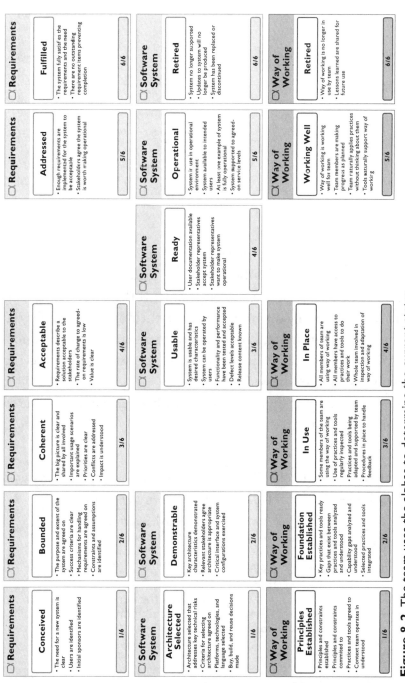

Figure 8-2 The team uses the alphas to determine the current states.

75

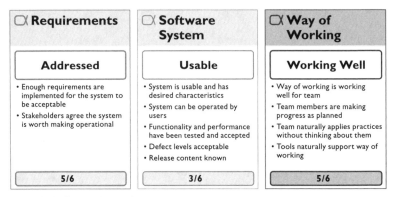

Figure 8-3 The selected next states

to first get to the Way of Working: Working Well state, then the Software System: Usable state, and finally the Requirements: Addressed state. The reason was simple: If their way of working did not work well, this would impede their attempts to get the software system usable. In addition, they agreed on the priority for the missing requirement items necessary to achieve the Requirements: Addressed state.

Smith and his team next discussed what needed to be done to achieve these states (see Table 8-2).

Table 8-2 How the Team Planned to Achieve the Selected Target States

Target State	How They Planned to Achieve Them
◻ **Way of Working** **Working Well** • Way of working is working well for team • Team members are making progress as planned • Team naturally applies practices without thinking about them • Tools naturally support way of working 5/6	Both Dick and Harriet agreed that they had difficulties in applying automated testing. They needed help in order to make progress. Tom agreed that he had to spend time teaching them. A task was added to the iteration backlog for Tom to conduct training on automated testing for Dick and Harriet.

Table 8-2 How the Team Planned to Achieve the Selected Target States (*continued*)

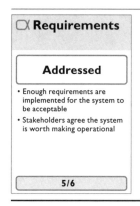

◻ Software System

Usable

- System is usable and has desired characteristics
- System can be operated by users
- Functionality and performance have been tested and accepted
- Defect levels acceptable
- Release content known

3/6

This state reminds us that the software system must be shown to be of sufficient quality and functionality to be useful to the users. So far, Smith's team had been testing within its development environment. Now it had to conduct tests within an acceptance test environment, which they had yet to prepare. This resulted in the following task:

Task 2. Prepare acceptance test environment.

Smith's team had to bring all requirement items currently demonstrable in the system to completion. By "complete" they meant that each requirement item must be fully tested within the acceptance test environment.

Task 3. Complete requirement item A: "Browse online and offline".

Task 4. Complete requirement item B: "Post comment (online and offline)".

Task 5. Complete requirement item C: "Browse album".

◻ Requirements

Addressed

- Enough requirements are implemented for the system to be acceptable
- Stakeholders agree the system is worth making operational

5/6

This state reminds us of the need to work with stakeholders to ensure that they are happy with the system produced. In our story Smith had to work with Angela to determine which additional requirement items needed to be implemented. This resulted in the following additional task:

Task 6: Talk to Angela and agree on additional requirement items, fitting in the iteration, to make the system worth being operational.

By going through the target alpha states, Smith was able to determine a set of objectives and tasks for the next iteration.

8.5 HOW THE KERNEL HELPS YOU IN PLANNING ITERATIONS

A good plan must be inclusive, meaning that it includes all essential items and covers the whole team. It must also be concrete, so it is actionable for the team. The team must also have a way to monitor its progress against the plan. The kernel helps you achieve this as follows.

- *Inclusive:* The kernel alphas serve as reminders across the different dimensions of software development, helping you to create a plan that addresses all dimensions in a balanced way.

- *Concrete:* The checklists for each alpha state give you hints as to what you need to do in the iteration. The same checklists help you determine your progress by making clear what you have done and comparing this to what you intended to do.

9

Doing and Checking the Iteration

In the preceding chapter we described how to plan an iteration using the kernel. At this point, the team has a set of tasks to perform to achieve the objectives of the iteration. These objectives and tasks form the team's iteration backlog. Each day in the iteration the team will take tasks from the iteration backlog and work on them. Work proceeds in this way until the end of the iteration when the team reviews what has been accomplished and determines the new state of the endeavor. The Plan-Do-Check-Adapt cycle repeats for each iteration. This chapter looks at how the kernel helps in the "doing and checking" part of the cycle.

9.1 DOING AND CHECKING THE ITERATION WITH THE KERNEL

In our story the team has chosen their own way of working, including working from an iteration backlog, holding daily meetings[1] to discuss their work, and working in short iterations.

---

1. Agile methods encourage teams to conduct daily meetings to discuss what each member has done since the previous meeting, what he or she is going to do that day, and potential impediments to progress. This helps each member understand what others are doing, and more importantly, provides a way for them to offer and get assistance from one another.

Daily meetings are often conducted in front of a task board. A task board in its simplest form categorizes tasks into three columns: "To Do", "Doing", and "Done". Task boards give teams a visual and quick overview of what the team is working on. One way the kernel can help is by enabling the objectives of the iteration to be placed onto the task board in the form of the desired target alpha states. This helps the team stay focused on the larger picture of the endeavor while working with the details.

Smith's team's task board had four columns, so the team could show their objectives alongside the progress of the tasks.

The "Objectives" column on the left of Figure 9-1 shows the target states Smith and his team selected as the objectives for their iteration. The "To Do" column shows the list of tasks planned for the iteration. In practice, these tasks are often written on sticky notes, and the state cards are printed on larger pieces of paper (as opposed to business card size) so that members can read and scribble on them easily.

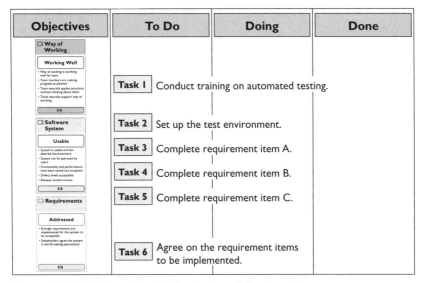

Figure 9-1 Task board at the beginning of the iteration

9.2 DOING AND CHECKING THE ITERATION IN OUR STORY

Let's look at how Smith and his team ran the iteration.

- *Day 1:* Figure 9-2 shows what happened on the first day of the iteration. Tom was conducting training on automated testing for his teammates (Task 1 in Figure 9-2). Tom was also setting up a test environment (Task 2 in Figure 9-2). Smith was discussing the requirement items to be implemented with Angela using the checklist items in the Requirements: Addressed state as a guide (Task 6 in Figure 9-2).

- *Day 2:* Figure 9-3 shows the task board on Day 2. Task 1 (conducting training on automated testing) was completed, but that did not mean the Way of Working was Working Well. Both Dick and Harriet needed to be fully up to speed on automated testing. Task 6 (agree on the requirement items to be implemented) was completed. This resulted

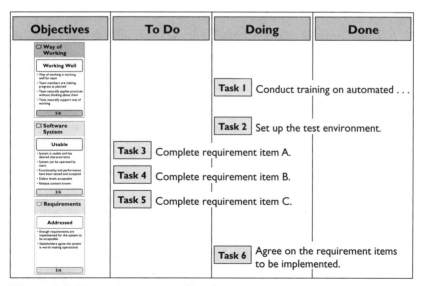

Figure 9-2 Doing the iteration: Day 1

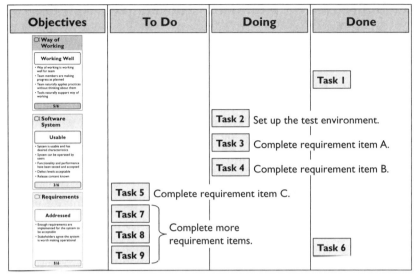

Figure 9-3 Doing the iteration: Day 2

in three new tasks, estimated to fit in the iteration, being added to the "To Do" column. Each of these tasks was about completing another requirement item.

- *Day 3:* On Day 3 of the iteration, Tom continued with Task 2. Dick worked on Task 3, and Harriet worked on Task 4. Smith was assisting the other team members in their respective tasks.

- *Day 4:* Figure 9-4 shows the task board on Day 4. Now, Tom had completed setting up the test environment. After working two days on Tasks 3 and 4, both Dick and Harriet had completed their requirement items. Angela had reviewed the results from the end user's point of view. Smith had also reviewed them from a technical point of view. Both Dick and Harriet had successfully applied automated testing. As such, the Way of Working: Working Well state was achieved, and its state card was moved to the "Done" column.

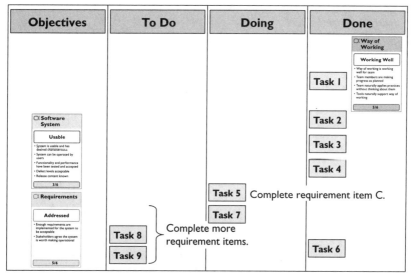

Figure 9-4 Doing the iteration: Day 4

On Day 4 of the iteration, Tom and Dick worked on Task 5 (complete requirement item C). Smith and Harriet worked on Task 7 (complete one of the new requirement items, which Smith and Angela identified on Day 1).

- *Day 6:* Figure 9-5 shows the task board two days later, on Day 6. Task 5 was completed. Now all requirement items that contributed to the software system being usable were implemented and reviewed. The team used the state checklist to help them evaluate whether or not the Software System was Usable. This resulted in the associated state card being moved to the "Done" column.

Now, at the end of Day 6 of the iteration, the team was still working on the remaining requirement items through Tasks 8 and 9.

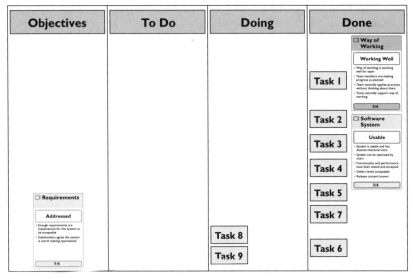

Figure 9-5 Doing the iteration: Day 6

9.3 HOW THE KERNEL HELPS YOU IN DOING AND CHECKING THE ITERATION

Maintaining focus is essential to achieving the agreed-on iteration objectives. Effective teams know when to say yes or no to additional work, and are always focusing on the most important things. The kernel alpha states with their checklists help the team to stay focused.

- *Iteration objectives:* Your team agrees on what the iteration objectives are. The alpha state checklists help your team agree on what needs to be done holistically.

- *Task prioritization:* If your team identifies or is given additional work, you should review the target alpha states' checklists to help determine if the new work is something you should prioritize now, or something that should be postponed.

- *Reminder for missing tasks:* Every day, your team will look at the checklists of the desired states. Ask yourself, "Do we have all the tasks we should be working on now?" In this way the checklists can help you identify missing tasks.

In this chapter we looked at how the kernel helps in doing and checking. In the next chapter we examine how the kernel helps you adapt your way of working.

10

Adapting the Way of Working

The kernel captures the essence of software engineering. It reminds you to involve your stakeholders, it reminds you to think about risk, and it helps you focus on the most important things now. Nonetheless, there will always be better ways of doing things. This chapter looks at how the kernel helps you adapt your way of working to suit your team.

10.1 ADAPTING THE WAY OF WORKING WITH THE KERNEL

Retrospectives are a great way to find out how to improve your way of working. Teams working iteratively do these at the end of every iteration. A typical way to run a retrospective is to have your team answer the following questions.

- What went well?
- What did not go well?
- What can be done better?

The way of working affects all team members, and every team member can contribute to it. This is another area where the kernel is useful. By talking about the alpha states at the retrospective, the team learns and can adapt the way that they move forward.

10.2 ADAPTING THE WAY OF WORKING IN THE STORY

Let's look at how Smith and his team ran the retrospective at the end of the iteration. Smith followed the common routine and asked the following questions.

- What went well?

- What did not go well?

- What can be done better?

At first, both Dick and Harriet were a little lost. Then Dick said, "Our application does what it needs to, but the user experience is not that good. Downloading is a little slow."

Dick was talking about the product, not their way of working. Smith tried to make the discussion more focused on the way of working by putting up the target alpha states of the iteration (see Figure 10-1).

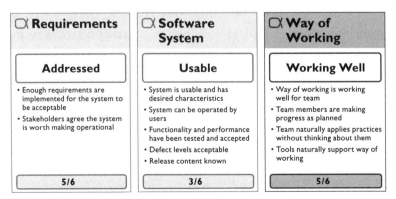

Figure 10-1 The target states of the iteration

Smith then asked the following questions.

- What went well with our planning, doing, and checking related to the previous alpha states?
- What did not go well with our planning, doing, and checking related to the previous alpha states?
- What can we do better with our planning, doing, and checking related to the previous alpha states?

Dick said, "Having Tom conduct training on automated testing for us went well."

Tom said, "The way you achieve the Requirements: Addressed state was not clear to me at the start of the iteration. I learned that I had to talk to Angela and get her to agree on the requirement items to be implemented. I didn't understand this just by looking at the state checklist."

Harriet said, "Actually, Smith, for me to do my job better I would like to have better guidance regarding how to work on a requirement item."

Smith considered Tom's request. That was easy; all Smith had to do was to supplement the state checklist with some additional guidance. He scribbled two lines of text onto the card as follows (see Figure 10-2).

- Gain agreement on requirement items that fall within the scope of Addressed.
- Implement these requirement items.

These notes were additional guidance on how to achieve the Addressed state.

Then Smith considered Harriet's request. This request was not as easy. It meant making the way of working on requirement

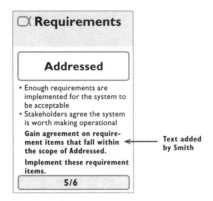

Figure 10-2 Guidance on achieving a state

items more explicit. We will discuss how to do this in the next chapter.

10.3 HOW THE KERNEL HELPS YOU IN ADAPTING THE WAY OF WORKING

The kernel helps you adapt your way of working in multiple ways.

10.3.1 Making the Way of Working Explicit

First, it allows you to make your way of working more explicit.

Developers who are just entering the workforce often know more about programming than developing software and more about developing software than working as a team and improving their way of working. Because their experience is limited, they often need a little help. The alphas and their states can help a team reason about their way of working as they try to improve it during a retrospective.

When conducting retrospectives, we make the alpha states visible to the team members to help them think about the "process" as opposed to the "product." If you are conducting an iteration retrospective, you only need to make visible those states that are relevant to the current iteration (i.e., the target states for the iteration). In this way, team members are not overwhelmed.

By visualizing the states, a mental transition takes place. The team is now looking at the "process." We then look at each state specifically, and ask the same questions.

- What went well during this iteration, and have we achieved this alpha state?

- What did not go well during this iteration, and do we know what is keeping us from achieving this alpha state?

- What can we do better in the next iteration that will help us achieve this alpha state?

10.3.2 Making Changes to the Way of Working

The daily contact your team has with the alpha states (and hence the kernel) helps you to find simple improvements to adapt your team's way of working. This may mean adding additional items to the alpha state checklist to meet your team's needs. Teams can also define new alphas. Such additions make the way of working more explicit, and hence provide better guidance to team members. How you extend the kernel elements is discussed briefly in the next chapter and looked at in depth in Part IV of this book.

Keep in mind that the team should only add information to the kernel elements and their checklist items. Changing the information that is already there would undermine the value that we gain through the use of a commonly agreed-on kernel.

11

Running an Iteration with Explicit Requirement Item States

The kernel alphas are very useful for guiding iterative development and helping development teams keep an eye on the big picture. However, some developers, such as Harriet in our story, may need more guidance on how to work.

11.1 WORKING WITH EXPLICIT REQUIREMENT ITEMS

You can adapt your way of working by introducing new alphas on top of the kernel. Actually, a Requirement Item is a kind of alpha, just like Requirements and Software System. Such an alpha can be added to provide guidance on how your team progresses through their requirement items. This is what Smith and his team decided to do.[1]

---

1. How to extend the kernel with specific elements and practices is explained later in the book.

After the retrospective, Smith and the team got together and defined a new Requirement Item alpha. To do this they discussed the life cycle of a typical requirement item, including the way they worked with their stakeholders to elicit their individual requirement items and agreed on their acceptance criteria, and how they built their iteration backlog and derived their development tasks. They also looked at the example kernel extensions provided by SEMAT to help teams add additional guidance as and when they need it. Figure 11-1 shows the requirement item they came up with.

The states were defined as follows.

1. *Identified:* A specific condition or capability that the software system must address has been identified.

   The requirement item has been identified, outlined, and approved by the team, including a customer representative.

2. *Described:* The requirement item is ready to be implemented.

   The team has agreed on the acceptance criteria with the customer representative, and has estimated the work needed to develop and test it. This clarifies what is needed and how much it will cost.

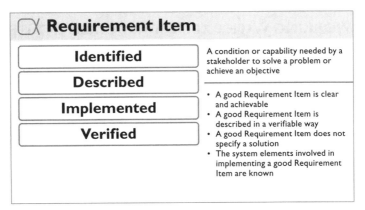

Figure 11-1 The new Requirement Item alpha and its states

3. *Implemented:* The requirement item is implemented in the software system and has been demonstrated to work.

   The developer(s) implementing the requirement item has completed all the coding and testing.

4. *Verified:* Successful implementation of the requirement item in the software system has been confirmed.

   Finally, the implementation of the requirement item has been reviewed and accepted by the team together with the customer representative, and is shown to meet the acceptance criteria. This signifies that work on the requirement item has been completed.

The team did this quite quickly as they found that they could base their requirement item definition on the generic example provided by SEMAT. They took the generic definition and related it to their way of working by qualifying the suggested states (Identified, Described, Implemented, and Verified) and adding explicit instructions on how they would achieve the states.

The team also captured a checklist for each requirement item state concisely on a state card (see Figure 11-2).

Requirement item states are very useful, especially when your requirement items take more than a few days to complete and your team needs more detailed tracking than discussed in the preceding chapter, where only tasks were tracked. The team could now use these new alphas as things to be progressed in the iteration and to refine the iteration backlog.

11.2 PLANNING AN ITERATION IN OUR STORY

Let's look at how Smith and his team run their next iteration using the explicit requirement item states.

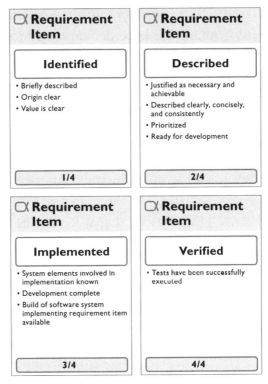

Figure 11-2 Requirement Item states

Smith and his team had already created a usable software system and were now incrementally adding requirement items. By now, the members of Smith's team were all familiar with the kernel. They determined the current state of development and the desired next states. Based on their discussion, they needed to get to the following alpha states:

- Requirements: Fulfilled
- Software System: Ready
- Way of Working: Working Well

To do this they had a number of requirement items[2] that they needed to complete, including the following.

- R1: Browse news feed offline.
- R2: Synchronize contents between device and social network.
- R3: Set synchronization and download policy.

The team recognized that once all these requirement items were completed (i.e., had reached the Verified state), they would have reached the Requirements: Fulfilled state and just have a little more work to do to get to the Software System: Ready state. In addition, if they progressed any of these requirement items to the final Verified state, they would have validated that they could run iterations with explicit requirement item states.

11.3 DOING ANOTHER ITERATION IN OUR STORY

Smith set up the task board with the completion of the relevant requirement items as clear objectives (see Figure 11-3).

Note the following, in particular.

- Smith placed the target kernel alpha states at the top of the "Objectives" column to help his team keep sight of the big picture.
- Smith placed a requirement item card into the "Objectives" column for each requirement item to be completed in the iteration.
- The requirement item cards showed all the states to remind the team that they needed to progress them, in a controlled manner, to the Verified state.

---

2. There were also other requirement items that we, to be brief, will not discuss (e.g., R4, R5).

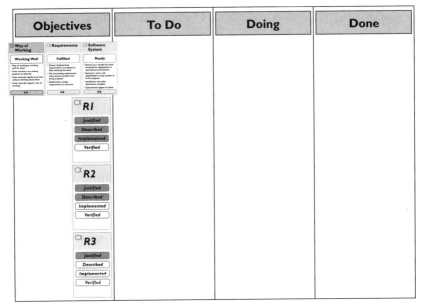

Figure 11-3 Smith's task board with requirement items

Before starting the iteration, the team assessed the state of each of their requirement items and indicated this by filling in the completed states on the cards. In this way, Figure 11-3 also shows the current state of each requirement item—R1, R2, and so on—at the beginning of this iteration. Figure 11-4 depicts this more clearly by shading the states that had already been achieved. For example, requirement item R1 had already been implemented and just needed to be verified.

Figure 11-4 Requirement item cards showing the current state

The team then added tasks to the task board to help them manage and track their work. For requirement item 1, which had already been implemented, there were only two tasks left to do.

- T1: Test R1.

- T2: Update end-user documentation.

These were two different tasks as they required different skill sets and could be done in parallel.

Just as with the kernel alphas, the states and the checklists helped the team to identify the tasks that needed to be done. For requirement item 2, which was in the Described state, three new tasks were needed.

- T3: Write the test cases and code needed to implement the requirement.

- T4: Test R2.

- T5: Complete the end-user documentation.

For requirement item 3 the team agreed that Smith and Angela needed to do some analysis before deciding how much work was necessary to complete the requirement item. So they just added one more task.

- T6: Analyze R3.

Once the analysis was complete, they would then add additional tasks to code, test, and document the changes needed to implement the requirement item in the next iteration. Figure 11-5 shows the task board at the end of the iteration planning.

The team then progressed the tasks in the same way as before, but this time they were able to see the individual requirement

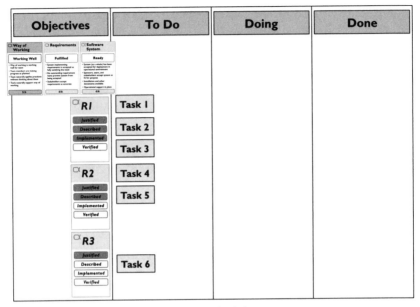

Figure 11-5 The task board at the end of the iteration

items being completed, and they updated the states as they were achieved.

After running the iteration, some requirement items were verified and others were still being worked on. This meant they achieved the Way of Working: Working Well state, even though the Requirements: Fulfilled state was not yet achieved. There were still open questions in relation to these requirement items, and the team agreed that they should get Angela's involvement to resolve them. Then they could plan how to address these requirement items in the next iteration.

11.4 ADAPTING THE WAY OF WORKING IN OUR STORY

At the end of the iteration, Smith facilitated a retrospective. In this iteration the team had targeted the Requirements: Fulfilled, Software System: Ready, and Way of Working: Working Well states. Smith highlighted these alpha states (see Figure 11-6).

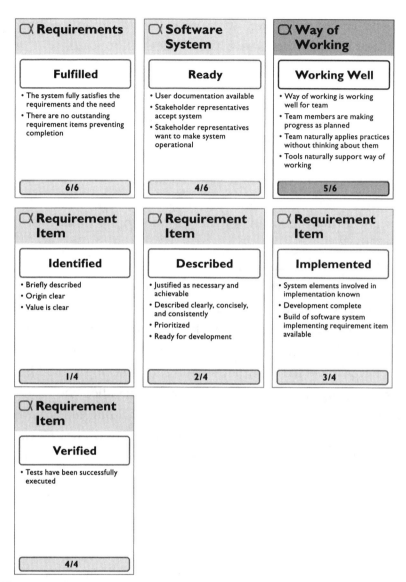

Figure 11-6 Conducting retrospectives, keeping the states visible

As before, Smith asked the following questions.

- What went well with our planning, doing, and checking related to the above alpha states?

- What did not go well with our planning, doing, and checking related to the above alpha states?

- What can we do better with our planning, doing, and checking related to the above alpha states?

Dick said, "When approaching the Requirement Item: Verified state we often find that Angela is looking for something slightly different. It is not easy to get her acceptance."

Harriet said, "We also seem to have built up quite a lot of defects during the testing of the system. I don't think that it is ready yet."

After some discussion, they agreed that they should get more involvement from Angela when working toward the second requirement item state, Described. After the retrospective, Smith took the feedback to Angela, and she agreed to work more closely with the team when working toward this state.

They also agreed that they should start tracking and addressing their bugs in the same way that they handled the requirement items. This led to the team adding a Bug alpha with a simple state machine (Detected, Located, Fixed, and Closed), which they could then use to set objectives and identify tasks. This also helped them to track how many open bugs they had as the iterations progressed.

11.5 DISCUSSION

In this chapter you saw an example demonstrating how the Requirement Item alpha can help a team stay focused on the most important things when working on their software. You also saw an example demonstrating how keeping the requirement item states visible to the team can help you track your progress and can help you see where your way of working might be improved.

FURTHER READING

Boehm, B. August 1986. "A Spiral Model of Software Development and Enhancement." ACM SIGSOFT Software Engineering Notes. *ACM* 11(4):14–24.

Bittner, K., and I. Spence. 2006. *Managing Iterative Software Development Projects* (Boston: Addison-Wesley).

Larman, C. 2003. *Agile and Iterative Development: A Manager's Guide* (Boston: Addison-Wesley).

Schwaber, K., and M. Beedle. 2008. *Agile Software Development with SCRUM* (Upper Saddle River, NJ: Prentice Hall).

Kniberg, H., and M. Skarin. 2010. *Kanban and Scrum: Making the Most of Both* (C4Media/InfoQ Enterprise Software Development Series).

PART III

USING THE KERNEL TO RUN A SOFTWARE ENDEAVOR

In Part II of the book we discussed how Smith's team ran a couple of iterations with the help of the kernel. In this part of the book we will demonstrate, through an expansion of the story used in Part II, how you can run a software endeavor through its full life cycle from idea to production. Through this story you will get a walkthrough of all the alpha states and how they help you conduct a software endeavor.

12

Running a Software Endeavor: From Idea to Production

In this chapter we will set the scene for our new story, and define what we mean by "from idea to production." In particular, we will show how a team can use the kernel within the constraints of its organization—specifically, its existing governance process.

12.1 THE PEOPLE IN OUR STORY AND CHALLENGES ALONG THE WAY

Let's start by briefly discussing the people in our story and the challenges they faced along the way.

Smith works with Angela in product planning/marketing. The company she works for provides mobile phones to the world market. Angela has come up with an idea for a new product, one that allows the caching of photos and other cloud-hosted data onto the phones themselves for offline viewing. Angela is the customer representative in our story. She doesn't understand how software is developed, and she doesn't understand or care about architecture.

Smith's teammate, Tom, is a hard-core coder who could solve almost any technical problem. But Tom could be a little myopic at times, jumping straight into code and losing sight of the big picture.

Fortunately, both Tom and Angela respected Smith and were open to discussing his recommendations in an objective manner.

Over the course of the development, the team would need to grow and would acquire two new teammates, Dick and Harriet. Dick, having come from a traditional waterfall development background, liked to be told exactly what to do. Harriet was inexperienced, having just finished school.

Angela, Smith, and the team all worked for Dave, who, as head of the Innovation Department, controlled the research budget and sat on the steering committee for all new-product development. It is Dave who eventually approved the team's plans and helped them secure the funding needed to develop the new product.

Dave's department built all of the company's software products. Before any of these software products could go live, they had to be handed over to the Production Department, which was responsible for the support, maintenance, and, most importantly, deployment of all the software that Dave's department produced.

As you can see, we are using the same application and the same team in this revision of the story, but this time we are looking at how the team would have progressed in a more formal and regulated business environment. We will be building on what you learned in Part II to use all the alphas rather than just focusing on Requirements, Software System, and Way of Working.

Of course, we understand that your situation is likely to be different from Smith's, but we do hope that the way Smith and his team overcame their challenges can shed light on how you can overcome yours by using the kernel to help guide your decisions.

12.2 UNDERSTANDING THE ORGANIZATIONAL CONTEXT

Within Smith's organization, all software development had to follow a standard governance process. Before funding was made available for the development of a new product, a business case and a high-level plan had to be prepared and submitted to the department's steering committee. The steering committee would then decide whether or not to go ahead with the development. This decision point was called the *Decision to Fund* and was an important milestone for every new software product.

The company was also very concerned about preserving its reputation for high-quality, innovative software products. To this end there was another important milestone to pass before a software system could be put into production. This second business decision point was called the *Decision to Go Live*.

The company's governance process is summed up in Figure 12-1, which shows the two milestones—Decision to Fund and Decision to Go Live—and where they appear in relationship to the work of the development team and their colleagues in production.

The story in this part of the book is divided into three chapters that reflect the evolution of the new software product—all the

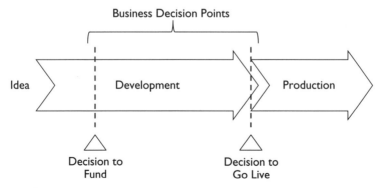

Figure 12-1 The two milestones in the company's governance process

way from idea to production. Each chapter shows how Smith's team or their colleagues achieve the next milestone.

- **Building the Business Case:** Angela had to prepare a business case and present it, along with a high-level plan, to the department's steering committee for approval. To place her ideas in context and create a credible plan, she immediately involved Smith and Tom from development. In Chapter 13 we will show how the kernel helped them to get started and create a compelling business case and a credible plan.

- **Developing the System:** Once the business case was funded and the development was approved, everything was ready to go and the team could start the iterative development of the software. In Chapter 14 we will revisit how the kernel helps the team to stay on track while developing good software.

- **Operating the Software:** Many development teams think the job is over once they release their software, or hand it over to another team for deployment and support. In Chapter 15 we will look at how the kernel can help these teams as well.

13

Building the Business Case

In this chapter we will walk through how Angela and the team built the business case for their new product. Creating good software is about more than writing high-quality code. Good software must be useful and of value to its stakeholders.

13.1 GETTING READY TO START IN OUR STORY

The story starts when Angela returns from her holiday with the idea for a new product. Knowing that the company would require her to build a business case to get funding to pursue her idea, Angela approached Smith and his team for help.

To help with the planning of the work and ensure that the team had the right short-term focus, Smith first mapped the governance decision points onto the kernel.

Using his state cards he identified what state each kernel alpha should be in at each milestone. The results, summarized in Figure 13-1, provided an initial road map to seed the plans.

This analysis helped Smith and Angela understand that they immediately needed to progress all three areas of concern.

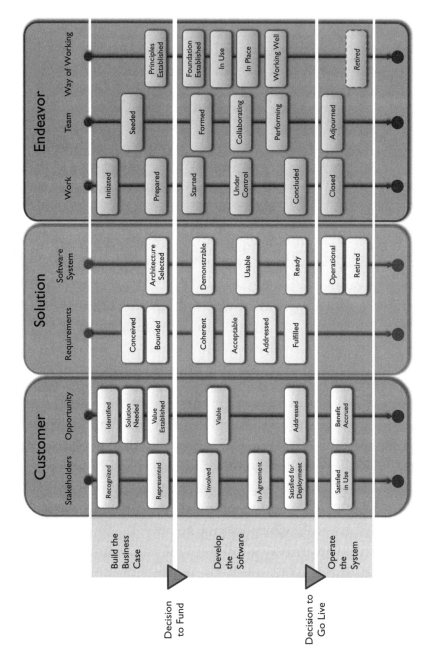

Figure 13-1 Aligning the kernel to the governance framework

- In the Customer area of concern they needed to progress both their understanding of the stakeholders and the opportunity. They needed to make sure their stakeholders were recognized and represented, and that the opportunity they had identified needed a solution and that this solution would be valued.

Analyzing what stakeholders need is often done without the participation of those who will implement and test the software. The stakeholder representatives do this analysis on their own, providing inputs to the development team once they have decided what they want. In this case Angela decided to involve Smith and the development team straight away, as she realized there was no point in getting over-excited about a potential new product if it couldn't be developed in a timely or cost-effective manner.

This meant progressing the Opportunity from Identified to Value Established and the Stakeholders from Recognized to Represented. It was in this area that Angela took the lead.

- In the Solution area of concern they needed to progress both their understanding of the requirements and their understanding of the proposed software system. They had seen too many projects fail because the business case was overly optimistic and did not set the right expectations by bounding the requirements or understanding the ramifications of their selected technologies. They certainly didn't want to document all the requirements, as this would have taken too long and wouldn't have helped the team progress at all. They just wanted to understand them well enough so that everyone could agree on the nature of the software system to be built.

In parallel with this they wanted to start thinking about the technology available and whether or not it was actually possible to build the kind of system Angela envisioned.

Smith recommended that they should at least evaluate the relevant technologies and select their initial architecture.

Because of this, they wanted to progress the Requirements to Bounded and the Software System to Architecture Selected before submitting the business case for approval. Angela and Smith worked together on the requirements, with Smith taking the lead for the software system.

- In the Endeavor area of concern they needed to make sure they had at least a coarse-grained estimate (a "guesstimate") and that they understood the approach the team would take.

Because of this, they wanted to progress the Work to the Prepared state and the Way of Working to the Foundation Established state. The team needed to be at the Seeded state. Although the key members of the team were already in place and fully committed to the product, they knew they would need additional team members to be able to successfully develop the product Angela desired.

Note

The Work alpha represents all the work the team needs to do to deliver on their commitments. It is the work that is organized into iterations and represented by the team's task board and plans. This doesn't mean that all the work needs to be broken down to a very detailed level at this time.

It was decided that Smith should take the lead here, as Angela wasn't qualified to plan the work, select the way of working, or build the team.

As shown in Figure 13-1, each milestone was aligned with the alpha states to remind the team what to emphasize at each stage of the endeavor. We will now look at what the team did to progress each area of concern.

13.2 UNDERSTANDING THE OPPORTUNITY AND THE STAKEHOLDERS

This is an essential part of understanding the market for any piece of software and is integral to the preparation of any business case. Let's look at how Angela, Smith, and the team achieved this.

The text in Table 13-1 is formatted into two columns. The column on the left shows the target alpha state with its key checklist items. The column on the right describes what the team did to progress the alpha. For brevity, we will not discuss all checklist items.

Table 13-1 How the Team Progressed the Alphas

State	How the State Was Achieved
☐ **Opportunity** **Identified** • Opportunity identified that could be addressed by a software-based solution • A stakeholder wishes to make an investment in better understanding potential value • Other stakeholders who share opportunity identified 1/6	Angela's job took her to many parts of the world. While in a restaurant, Angela tried to show her friends some photos from her Facebook profile, but there was no Internet connection. She was frustrated. Having offline access to your social network is important. Angela believed that if a mobile service could have such a capability, it would clearly differentiate the service from its competition. Through her research, Angela discovered that most social network apps assume a reliable network connection. So she concluded that she had identified a real business opportunity.
☐ **Stakeholders** **Recognized** • Stakeholders have been identified • There is agreement on stakeholder groups to be represented • Responsibilities of stakeholder representatives defined 1/6	Angela could not simply tell developers in her company to work immediately on her idea. She had to get agreement from colleagues in her department and from her boss, Dave. Together they considered her idea from the perspective of different kinds of users, and they evaluated the idea.

continues

Table 13-1 How the Team Progressed the Alphas (*continued*)

State	How the State Was Achieved
☐ **Stakeholders** **Represented** • Stakeholder representatives appointed • Stakeholder representatives agree to take on responsibilities and are authorized to do so • Collaboration approach agreed on • Representatives respect team's way of working **2/6**	Angela's department had regular monthly product planning meetings where they discussed product ideas. In this way, everyone got their ideas and comments heard and debated. Those invited to the monthly product planning meetings represented all the stakeholders in the department, and they were given the responsibility and authority to review and make decisions on the direction the product would take.
☐ **Opportunity** **Solution Needed** • Need for software-based solution confirmed • Stakeholders' needs identified • Underlying problem and root causes identified • At least one software-based solution proposed **2/6**	During the product planning meeting, Angela presented her idea. She explained how often people find themselves in places without Internet connections when they have a real need to access their social network. The idea was then discussed in detail. Dave as well as Angela's other colleagues agreed that the idea was a good one and that a software-based solution could solve the root cause of the problem.
☐ **Opportunity** **Value Established** • The value of a successful solution established • Impact of solution on stakeholders understood • Value of software system understood **3/6**	Angela's department discussed her idea further. They agreed that it would be a valuable differentiator compared to other similar services. In fact, it was believed that it could double the sales of their new phone, which was failing to get its predicted share of the market. Moreover, it would be well positioned for their next-generation mobile devices, whose target audience was frequent travelers. As the department head, Dave gave the go-ahead.

What can go wrong here? How can the kernel help you?

It is important to get the stakeholders and the developers on the same page with a shared understanding of the product and the responsibilities each of them will have during the product's development. In our story there was a forum in place for Angela to discuss and refine her ideas together with the stakeholders. What if you do not have such a forum to discuss ideas? The kernel will remind you of the importance of setting one up and making sure the right people are involved. If they question the value of the forum, you can use the kernel to help them understand why this is important by discussing the alpha states and checklist items as described in this chapter.

What types of challenges are you likely to face? A few examples include the following.

- Is the idea unclear?
- Are the stakeholders not involved?
- Is the solution unclear?
- Are the requirements unclear?

The kernel helps you by highlighting what questions to ask and what actions to take to keep your endeavor on track.

13.3 UNDERSTANDING THE SOLUTION

While they were working to understand the stakeholders and the value of the proposed product, Smith, Tom, and Angela were also working to build their understanding of their proposed solution.

Table 13-2 explains how they bounded the requirements and selected the architecture for the software system.

Table 13-2 How the Team Bounded the Requirements and Selected the Architecture

State	How the State Was Achieved
⊂⟨ Requirements **Conceived** • The need for a new system is clear • Users are identified • Initial sponsors are identified 1/6	Angela wrote a brief overview describing the application, including who the expected users and customers would be and how the application would benefit them.
⊂⟨ Requirements **Bounded** • The purpose and extent of the system are agreed on • Success criteria are clear • Mechanisms for handling requirements are agreed on • Constraints and assumptions are identified 2/6	Angela gave to Smith and Tom an overview of what the application was about. They brainstormed the key requirement items that were necessary in order to have a useful application. The agreed-on list of requirement items included the following. • Browse profile (online and offline). • Browse news feed (online and offline). • Browse album (online and offline). • Browse videos (online and offline). • Post comments (online and offline). • Synchronize contents between device and social network. • Set synchronization and download policy.
⊂⟨ Software System **Architecture Selected** • Architecture selected that addresses key technical risks • Criteria for selecting architecture agreed on • Platforms, technologies, and language selected • Buy, build, and reuse decisions made 1/6	Smith and Tom started investigating the architecture for the application. The application was small, but they still had the following architecture issues to resolve: • The caching mechanism (how much to cache and how to cache) • The caching policy (when to update the cache, what to cache, etc.) • How to integrate with their existing application for browsing social networks in an online mode Through discussion and prototyping, they found some candidate solutions and agreed on which solution they preferred.

What can go wrong here? How can the kernel help you?

By taking the time to understand the type of system to be built and investigating the technologies available, the team significantly de-risked the project and provided their business case with some much needed credibility. Teams often forget to assess the viability of their ideas, placing too much emphasis on the early detailing of the requirements before selecting or exploring the architectural issues.

In the early stages of development the kernel reminds you to balance your objectives, and the alpha states and checklists help you reach an appropriate level of detail.

13.4 PREPARING TO DO THE WORK

The team also needed a plan to support the business case. They didn't need a detailed plan of all their expected activities, but they did need a schedule, an effort estimate, and most importantly, a release plan showing when the product would be released to the market.

Table 13-3 highlights how they prepared to do the work and established the principles behind their intended way of working.

Table 13-3 How the Team Prepared the Work and Established the Principles behind Their Way of Working

State	How the State Was Achieved
⨉ Team **Seeded** • Team's mission is clear • Team knows how to grow to achieve mission • Required competencies are identified • Team size is determined 1/5	Dave agreed that Smith and Tom should work together with Angela to prepare the plans and the business case. Smith and Tom were competent developers who had experience in mobile application development. Dave told Smith that if he needed additional team members to let him know.

continues

Table 13-3 How the Team Prepared the Work and Established the Principles behind Their Way of Working (*continued*)

State	How the State Was Achieved
α Work **Initiated** • Work initiator known • Work constraints clear • Sponsorship and funding model clear • Priority of work clear 1/6	Angela and Dave shared with Smith and Tom what the opportunity was about, and they discussed the emerging requirements. With that, development started. Even though Angela would be very much involved in preparing the business case, the responsibility to drive the development work was now with Smith and Tom. They set a date for the completion of the business case. Dave gave them a month to get ready.
α Work **Prepared** • Cost and effort estimated • Funding and resources to start work in place • Acceptance criteria understood • Governance procedures agreed on • Risk exposure understood • Dependencies clear 2/6	Smith and Tom knew they needed a high-level plan to establish the budget and resources needed for the development.
α Way of Working **Principles Established** • Principles and constraints established • Principles and constraints commited to • Practices and tools agreed to • Context team operates in understood 1/6	Smith and Tom agreed that they would run the development using the following practices: • Iterative development • Test-driven development • Continuous integration

What can go wrong here? How can the kernel help you?

Early in any development the challenge for a team is always to balance the need to prepare—that is, to understand the opportunity, capture some requirements, and plan the project—with the need to start developing software as soon as possible. The classic mistakes are always to either (1) err too much on the side of caution and front-load the project with too much preparatory work documenting all the requirements and planning every aspect of the work, or (2) not doing any planning and preparation work at all.

The kernel helps you balance all these forces by understanding where you and the team are in each dimension of software development. This allows you to openly discuss and decide where you should be at any time in the evolution of the software system.

13.5 ESTABLISHING A HIGH-LEVEL PLAN

Although we have now walked through all the alpha states involved in building the business case, it is worth taking a little more time to look at how Smith and the team planned their work.

The first thing Smith did was to get the team to agree on some intermediate milestones to place between the two mandated ones: the Decision to Fund and the Decision to Go Live. Smith's reasoning here was to start fleshing out a plan so that he could get a handle on how difficult and time-consuming the work might be.

The team agreed that the system should be developed incrementally by first developing what Smith called a *skinny system*. This is a minimal implementation of the final system that implements a small number of the key requirements to prove the architecture. It would also allow the team to get confirmation of what's really wanted. The stakeholders would use this skinny system to understand the application and to clarify their requirements. To represent when this skinny system would be available they added a new milestone called Skinny System Available to the plan.

They also agreed that they should then build on the skinny system to create a production-quality system—one that implemented enough of the requirements to provide a minimal but complete solution—as soon as possible. This gave them a second new milestone, Usable System Available.

Finally, they would evolve this into the final system and prepare it to hand over to the production team at the Decision to Go Live milestone.

Using their state cards the team started to select the alpha states that should be achieved at each of the two new milestones, starting with the cards for the Software System, Requirements, and Stakeholders (see Figure 13-2). By working in this way they realized it was important to gain the agreement of the stakeholders by the time the skinny system was available, as without this agreement there would be no evidence that they had built the right skinny system.

To help keep things in balance and show their overall intentions they also aligned the expectation for progress in the other areas of the kernel to these new milestones. This resulted in an update to the overall plan (see Figure 13-3) where the two new milestones are added to provide interim checkpoints during the development of the software.

At the Skinny System Available milestone the team needs to prepare the skinny system and reach agreement with the stakeholders. This milestone will still be achieved if the team is not collaborating and the way of working is not fully in place, but it can certainly be argued that if these other goals have not been achieved the chances of quickly producing an effective skinny

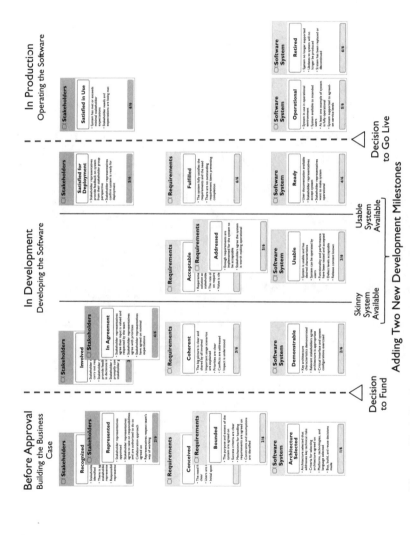

Figure 13-2 Defining the milestones with state card

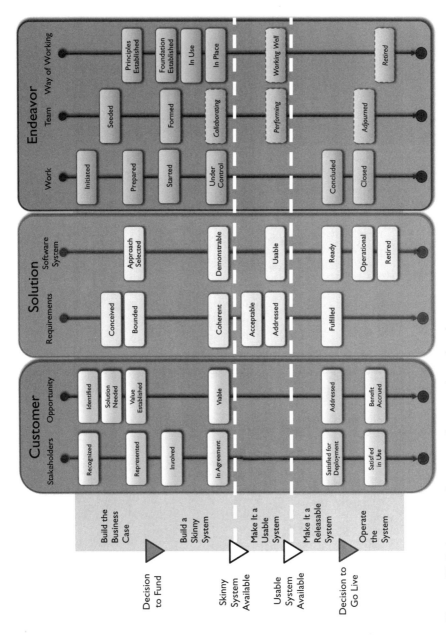

Figure 13-3 Inserting the new milestones into the plan

system are greatly reduced. So the key here is for the team to progress the Stakeholders, Requirements, and Software System while keeping an eye on the progress of the Opportunity, Work, Team, and Way of Working.

The states that the team desires to achieve at a particular milestone, but that are not essential to pass the milestone, are shown in italics with a dashed outline in Figure 13-3 and in all the following diagrams used to illustrate the team's milestones.

13.6 BUILDING THE SCHEDULE

As part of the evolving plan, the team needed to provide a schedule and rough estimate for the delivery of the new system. Based on the emerging requirements and the results of the early prototyping, Smith and the team decided they were prepared to commit to delivering the first release six months after the decision to fund the development was taken.

The team's approach to development is iterative. Figure 13-4 shows an overview of the team's schedule.

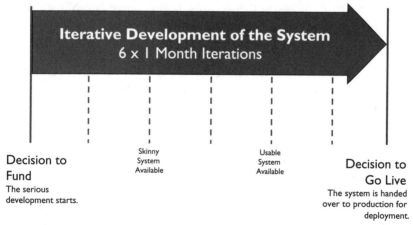

Figure 13-4 The team's schedule

The vertical dashed lines in Figure 13-4 represent the boundary between iterations. Each iteration was one month in length and was run using the Plan-Do-Check-Adapt cycle discussed in Part II of this book.

Due to the risk and complexity inherent in the new system, the team decided it would probably take them two iterations to create the skinny system and a further two iterations to achieve a usable system. The final two iterations would be used to add as much functionality to the system as possible, and prepare the system for delivery to production. The team understood that the more successful the early iterations were the more functionality they would be able to deliver. Alternatively, if things went well they might be able to go live earlier than scheduled. Adapting the plans to reflect the progress made by the team is a fundamental principle of any iterative approach and was fully embraced by the team.

Note that getting to a certain state, or set of states, does not necessarily coincide with the end of any particular iteration. An alpha state might take several iterations to achieve, and an iteration might move a particular alpha through several states. For example, some of the states required to achieve the Skinny System Available milestone could be achieved at the end of the first iteration and some of the others midway through the second. The key thing is that the team expected to have achieved all the necessary progress by the end of the second iteration.

Smith's team also discussed whether or not they should come up with a more detailed plan for the development. The consensus was that they should at least identify which requirement items and technical issues they should have addressed by the next milestone. They could then estimate these and use the estimates to check the credibility of the plan.

The next milestone was to develop a skinny system. After discussing this with Angela, they agreed on the following scope for the skinny system.

- Architecture issues to be resolved:
  - Caching mechanism
  - Caching policy
  - Integration with the existing system
- Requirement items to be demonstrated:
  - Browse profile offline; basic functionality
  - Browse album offline; basic functionality
  - Synchronize contents between device and social network; basic functionality

The team referred to the chosen requirement items as architecturally significant because once they were implemented there would be sufficient evidence that the critical architecture issues were resolved. Angela, Smith, and Tom also discussed what should be achieved by the Usable System Available milestone and thought that the following would probably be enough:

- Browse profile offline; full functionality
- Browse album offline; full functionality
- Synchronize contents between device and social network; full functionality
- Set synchronization and download policy

Angela and Smith agreed that allocating the preceding milestones to the next two milestones would be sufficient to get the team going. They would refine the plan as the development proceeded.

13.7 HOW THE KERNEL HELPS YOU IN GETTING STARTED

In this chapter, we have demonstrated three important uses of the kernel.

13.7.1 Embracing Your Stakeholders

As a software professional, you have a responsibility to create good software. You also need to know you are working on what matters most to the stakeholders: the things that are truly going to deliver value. As a software professional, you can use the checklists associated with your current state to help guide your decisions and to remind you to ask questions when you sense uncertainty or risk. For example, checklist items in the Opportunity alpha remind you to ask your stakeholders the following questions.

- What is the opportunity?
- Is the solution needed?
- Are there other stakeholder groups we should be talking to?

Asking such questions can help you understand the real need that the software system should fulfill.

13.7.2 Guiding Development

There is no single life cycle and high-level plan that fits all development endeavors. With the kernel, you have the building blocks to define your own life cycle and high-level plan. The building blocks are the alpha states. You define the life cycle and develop your high-level plan by aligning the alpha states to your chosen milestones. In our story, the development life cycle and high-level plan chosen by our team is one that attacks architecture risks first. There are other approaches where requirements are detailed and baselined before starting actual development. Defining your approach using the kernel will be discussed in a little more detail in Section 18.2.

The benefit of using the kernel to guide your planning is that you can associate progress in different dimensions of software development to your milestone definitions.

13.7.3 Planning Ahead

One of the greatest challenges observed on many software endeavors is coming up with a realistic plan that has the right level of detail to enable your team to best meet the opportunity in a timely fashion and to get support from the stakeholders. How does the kernel help? The kernel helps you reason about how far you can plan ahead and to what level of detail. By planning, we mean associating the agreed-on life-cycle milestones with definite achievements (e.g., which requirement items need to be completed and by when).

Planning ahead doesn't mean planning everything that is going to happen, but rather being aware of your goal and how you are going to get there. You can use the kernel to help you decide what you need to progress by when, as well as understanding where you are at any point in time. The order in which you tackle the challenges you face is dependent on the business context that the system is developed in, and the experiences of the people involved. The kernel is supportive of evolutionary development, continuous development, and other, more front-loaded waterfall approaches. It is also useful when reasoning about the effectiveness of these and any other approaches in your toolkit.

In this chapter we walked through how the team built the business case for their new product. In the next chapter we discuss how the team developed their system.

14

Developing the System

In this chapter we will discuss how Smith's team developed their system. Developing software is extremely challenging because, as we discussed in Chapter 1, it is multidimensional—there are risks and challenges in different dimensions: opportunity, requirements, software system, and so forth. At different points in time and on different software endeavors, the emphasis needed on each dimension will vary. Together, a development team must have skills across all these dimensions and must understand how they interact to ensure that each one gets appropriate attention.

This chapter describes how Smith's team dealt with the different dimensions in parallel while building a high-quality system for deployment by their colleagues in production. This chapter focuses on the period between the Decision to Fund and the Decision to Go Live milestones, the area of the plan highlighted in Figure 14-1.

The sections in this chapter describe how Smith's team worked toward each milestone in their plan. In each section we look at what the team did to progress each area of concern: Customer, Solution, and Endeavor.

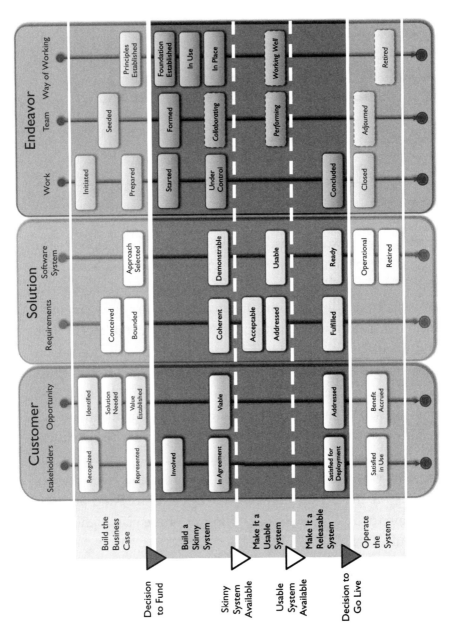

Figure 14-1 Developing the system

- **Building the Skinny System—Getting Things Working**

  1. **Engaging the stakeholders:** The team felt it was important to get the stakeholders involved to make sure they agreed that the team was creating something useful.

  2. **Starting development:** The team's main focus was on producing a skinny system to validate the selected architecture; one that has the ability to grow to become the system to be delivered. This forced the team to exercise their way of working, and provide real evidence of whether or not the goals are achievable and the opportunity is viable.

  3. **Establishing an agreed-on way of working:** The team needed to be sure they had a usable development environment and an agreed-on way of working.

- **Making the Skinny System Usable—Getting Things Working Well**

  1. **Keeping the stakeholders involved:** The team wanted to involve their stakeholders in all stages of the development to make sure they produced the best system they could. Although there were no state changes planned for the Stakeholders and Opportunity alphas during these iterations, the team knew it was essential to actively monitor their health.

  2. **Evolving a usable system:** Once the architecture was validated, the development team intended to incrementally add functionality to make the system not just demonstrable but actually usable.

  3. **Getting to a good way of working:** The development team wanted to become a truly high-performance team and continuously improve. They made sure their plans included time to tune their way of working, adapt their

plans, and properly integrate the new team members into the team.

- **Evolving a Deployable Solution—Concluding the Work**

  1. **Gaining acceptance:** An important part of the Decision to Go Live milestone was to have the stakeholders sign off on the final acceptance of the system produced. Once the software system was ready, the stakeholders and the development team worked together to achieve acceptance.

  2. **Getting to delivery:** Once the system was usable, the development team incrementally added functionality to the system, always ensuring that it was of good quality and remained usable. Additional support material and quality checks are often needed before a system is deemed to be ready. In this case a number of standard performance and security checks had to be passed by the release candidate before the system could be released to production.

  3. **Done! Completing development work:** Finally, the software system was handed over for deployment. The team didn't know if they would continue to work on the product, or if Dave would assign them all to other work. Regardless of this, the team would conclude the development work and run a final retrospective for the endeavor.

Note that what we describe here is just how Smith's team decided to run the development of the first release of a brand-new system. The way you decide to run yours will likely be different, and your development effort may not go as smoothly as this simple example. The kernel's greatest value is in guiding you when things don't go smoothly and you have difficult decisions to make.

We cannot explain in this short book all the situations you might face, but we can provide a few examples to help you learn the idea. These examples are provided in the following sections. As in Chapter 13, each section looks at what the team did in each of the three areas of concern.

14.1 BUILDING THE SKINNY SYSTEM—GETTING THINGS WORKING

The team agreed to use their first two iterations to prove their architecture, further engage with their stakeholders, and test their approach.

The goal was to achieve the Skinny System Available milestone, which is summarized in Figure 14-2.

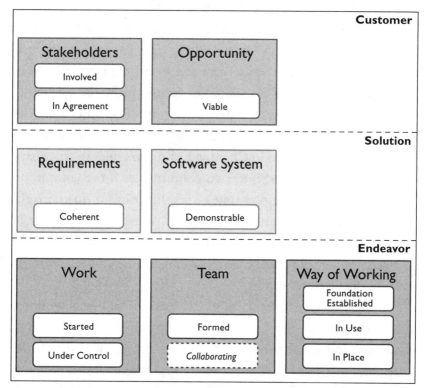

Figure 14-2 The team's first development milestone

- In the Customer area of concern it was all about getting the stakeholders engaged and making sure they were in agreement that the opportunity was viable.

- In the Solution area of concern it was all about producing a demonstrable, skinny version of the system to prove the architecture. For this to be achieved the requirements themselves needed to be coherent, as otherwise there would be no context for the testing of the architecture.

- In the Endeavor area of concern it was all about bringing the work under control, making sure an appropriate team was formed (and preferably collaborating), and an appropriate way of working was in place.

14.2 ENGAGING THE STAKEHOLDERS

It is important to get stakeholders involved in the development to ensure that the team is always working on what is most important. The stakeholders themselves need to be in agreement about the opportunity being pursued, the requirements being implemented, and the software system being produced. Let's look at Table 14-1 and see how Angela, Smith, and the team achieved this. (As with the tables in Chapter 13, in the tables in this chapter the text is formatted into two columns, with the column on the left showing the alpha states and the column on the right describing what the team did to achieve or maintain the state.)

What can go wrong here? How can the kernel help you?

The goal here is to make sure the endeavor is aligned with the stakeholders from the start.

So, what happens when you go off track? The kernel will help you. For example, the kernel reminds you of the importance of achieving and maintaining stakeholder agreement through the checklists in the Stakeholders and Opportunity states. This is reinforced by the checklists for the other alphas and their states, such as those for the Software System: Demonstrable state and the Software System: Usable state. So, if you do go off track the kernel will help you detect it.

Table 14-1 How the Team Engaged the Stakeholder

State	How the State Was Achieved
Stakeholders **Involved** • Stakeholder representatives carry out responsibilities • Stakeholder representatives provide feedback and take part in decisions in timely way • Stakeholder representatives promptly communicate to stakeholder group 3/6	Angela made herself available for the team when they had questions to ask. She also made it a point to provide proactive feedback to the team when needed. Angela also communicated the team's progress to the other stakeholders via the monthly product planning meetings.
Opportunity **Viable** • A solution has been outlined • Indications are solution can be developed and deployed within constraints • Risks are manageable. 4/6	At the beginning of the development, Smith and his team had drafted an initial plan. As the work progressed, Smith and Angela updated the plan regularly and shared this with the other stakeholders. The production and demonstration of the skinny system provided enough evidence that the plan was credible and that a solution could be produced within the cost and schedule constraints.
Stakeholders **In Agreement** • Stakeholder representatives agree their input is valued and respected by the team • Stakeholder representatives agree with priorities • Stakeholder representatives have agreed on minimal expectations 4/6	After the successful demonstration of the skinny system, Angela prioritized the requirement items based on what she heard from all the other stakeholders. She also worked with Smith to define which requirement items would make it to the final version of the system. Smith listened to all of Angela's concerns and requested clarification in areas where the team didn't fully understand what was needed.

14.3 STARTING DEVELOPMENT

As well as engaging their stakeholders the team focused most of their attention on producing a skinny system. This skinny system would

- Implement some key requirement items
- Validate the architecture
- Be able to grow to accommodate other requirement items without significant rework

To achieve this they also had to agree in detail with Angela on what the requirement items targeted for the skinny system really meant (see Table 14-2).

Table 14-2 How the Team Started Development

State	How the State Was Achieved
☐ **Requirements** **Coherent** • The big picture is clear and shared by all involved • Important usage scenarios are explained • Priorities are clear • Conflicts are addressed • Impact is understood 3/6	Smith worked with Angela to clarify the key requirements by writing acceptance test cases for them. In doing so, they started to realize that some requirement items were either duplicated or similar to one another. So they refined and consolidated the requirement items, and prioritized them.
☐ **Software System** **Demonstrable** • Key architecture characteristics demonstrated • Relevant stakeholders agree architecture is appropriate • Critical interface and system configurations exercised 2/6	Meanwhile, Tom, Dick, and Harriet were implementing the first requirement items. Both Smith and Tom reviewed the team's test cases to make sure all critical interfaces had been tested. Eventually, they had a version of the system that they could show Angela and the other stakeholder representatives. The stakeholders agreed that the key architecture characteristics were being addressed.

What can go wrong here? How can the kernel help you?

The goal here was to validate the architecture to ensure that it addressed the technical challenges, and that it provided the foundation for the software system to grow gracefully. The team achieved this through building an initial version of the system, called the skinny system, which exercised all the important characteristics of the system. Since the skinny system was small, it was relatively easy to test and change. Once the skinny system met its criteria, incorporating the remaining requirement items was unlikely to cause any major problems.

Some teams are unable to limit the scope of the skinny system, and thus they spend significant effort before they can validate the architecture. In the worst case, the team might be validating the architecture for the first time when the system is nearly completed. This is very risky because late changes to the architecture are likely to cause delays and dissatisfied stakeholders.

The kernel itself does not provide concrete guidance on how to build a skinny system, but it reminds you of the importance of doing so. The kernel also indicates that you do not need to reach all the requirements to build the skinny system. You only need to get to the Requirements: Coherent state to determine what should be in the skinny system.

14.4 ESTABLISHING AN AGREED-ON WAY OF WORKING

From the start, Smith and Tom recognized that it was important to get the development environment in place and to get the team members on board and working well together (see Table 14-3).

What can go wrong here? How can the kernel help you?

The goal here is to get the way of working in place so that each team member knows how to collaborate and work together. Coming to an agreement on the way of working is not easy.

Table 14-3 How the Team Established an Agreed-on Way of Working

State	How the State Was Achieved
◘ **Way of Working** — **Foundation Established** — • Key practices and tools ready • Gaps that exist between practices and tools analyzed and understood • Capability gaps analyzed and understood • Selected practices and tools integrated — **2/6**	Smith and Tom started to set up their development and test environment, which included • A code repository • An integrated development environment • A mobile device emulator • A continuous integration tool They also selected a collaboration and task management tool that they had used on a previous software endeavor.
◘ **Work** — **Started** — • Development work has started • Work progress is monitored • Work broken down into actionable items with clear definition of done • Team members are accepting and progress work items — **3/6**	In parallel to preparing their way of working Smith and Tom also started the development work. They analyzed the requirement items with the highest priority, and wrote code and test cases. They started to make use of their development environment and follow their way of working.
◘ **Way of Working** — **In Use** — • Some members of the team are using the way of working • Use of practices and tools regularly inspected • Practices and tools being adapted and supported by team • Procedures in place to handle feedback — **3/6**	At this point in time Smith and Tom were exercising the way of working by using the tools and working on the agreed-on requirement items.

Table 14-3 How the Team Established an Agreed-on Way of Working (*continued*)

State	How the State Was Achieved
⊃ Team **Formed** • Team has enough resources to start the mission • Team organization and individual responsiblities understood • Members know how to perform work 2/5	The new developers, which Smith had requested, had just joined the team. These two developers were Dick and Harriet. They had different backgrounds and experiences. Smith walked through the work principles, practices, and key tools to familiarize them with the team's way of working. Smith also set up a team kickoff meeting to make sure all the team members shared Angela's vision.
⊃ Way of Working **In Place** • All members of team are using way of working • All members have access to practices and tools to do their work • Whole team involved in inspection and adaptation of way of working 4/6	Through guidance from Smith and Tom, both Dick and Harriet got familiar with the team's way of working, the development environment, and the practices. And they began using the way of working to do their tasks.
⊃ Team **Collaborating** • Members working as one unit • Communication is open and honest • Members focused on team mission • Success of team ahead of personal objectives 3/5	The two iterations went well, and by the end of the second iteration all members were working together, focusing on the team's mission and helping one another address any problems as they occurred. Reaching this state often takes significant time with a newly formed team. Smith and Tom worked closely with Dick and Harriet, answering their questions about the team's way of working and development environment. They also found they had to frequently remind the new members of the team's objectives when they would start to drift off-course.

continues

Table 14-3 How the Team Established an Agreed-on Way of Working (*continued*)

State	How the State Was Achieved
⊃ Work **Under Control** • Work going well, risks being managed • Unplanned work and rework under control • Work items completed within estimates • Measures tracked 4/6	As we discussed in Part II of the book, Smith and his team tracked the progress of their objectives, requirement items, and tasks. They made this visible to all team members, including Angela. In this way, everyone on the team knew how much work they had to do, and how much work was left in each iteration. By the end of the second iteration the way of working was in place, the team was collaborating, and the skinny system had successfully passed its tests. Based on these results the team was able to fine-tune their plans, and confidently confirm their commitments to their stakeholders.

Team members typically have different opinions based on their personal experience and preferences.

Agreeing on a way of working can be quite philosophical. A good way to reach an initial agreement is to walk through the development approach and ask the team if they know what they should do at each step. The kernel can guide you in this walk-through by using the alpha states to touch on all key dimensions.

After reaching an initial agreement on the way of working, you should continuously improve it through retrospectives. Only real use of the way of working can tell you what really needs to be changed or improved. As we saw in Part II, the kernel can help with this, too.

Note that not all of the state changes are necessary for the team to progress. As we discussed in Chapter 13, the states shown in italics on the road map (see Figure 13-3 in that chapter) are things the team expected to achieve in synchronization with the other states, but were not as essential. In this case the team members were collaborating well with one another by the time they reached the Skinny System Available milestone, but it wouldn't have been the end of the world if they weren't, and it certainly wouldn't have prevented them from achieving their stated goal of building and demonstrating a skinny system.

14.5 MAKING THE SKINNY SYSTEM USABLE— GETTING THINGS WORKING WELL

The team agreed to use their next two iterations to evolve the system from demonstrable to usable. This meant completing the functionality demonstrated by the skinny system, and incrementally adding the functionality to provide a minimal but complete system.

The goal was to achieve the Usable System Available milestone, which is summarized in Figure 14-3.

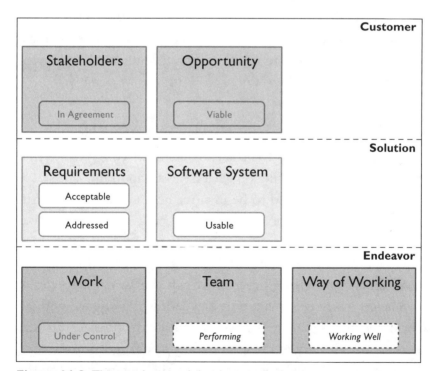

Figure 14-3 The team's second development milestone

- In the Customer area of concern it was all about keeping the stakeholders involved and making sure they were still in agreement that, given the progress made by the team and any changes in the marketplace, the opportunity was still viable. As this is all about maintaining the health of the Stakeholders and Opportunity states rather than explicitly progressing them, these states are shown grayed out in Figure 14-3.

- In the Solution area of concern it was all about maturing the Requirements and Software System states. Angela and Dave wanted the system to not just be usable, but be usable enough that it could be deployed if necessary. To this end the requirements needed to be acceptable and enough of them implemented that the stakeholders agreed that they were addressed.

- In the Endeavor area of concern it was all about maintaining control over the work being done and improving the team's performance. The plan was for the team to go beyond just collaborating and to really start performing, and in the process show that their way of working was working well.

14.6 KEEPING THE STAKEHOLDERS INVOLVED

It is important to keep the stakeholders involved to ensure that the team is always working on what is most important. The stakeholders themselves need to be in agreement about the opportunity being pursued, the requirements being implemented, and the software system being produced. Let's look at Table 14-4 and see how Angela, Smith, and the team achieved this.

What can go wrong here? How can the kernel help you?

The goal here is to make sure the endeavor is aligned with all the other things that are happening outside the project. It is very easy for the viability of the opportunity to change, or to be lost, because of changing priorities within the organization or the actions of competitors. By monitoring the health of the opportunity and continuously working with the stakeholders, you can balance the progress made by the team with the ever-changing situation in the market.

Table 14-4 How the Team Kept the Stakeholders Involved

State	How the State Was Maintained
⊠ Stakeholders **Involved** • Stakeholder representatives carry out responsibilities • Stakeholder representatives provide feedback and take part in decisions in timely way • Stakeholder representatives promptly communicate to stakeholder group 3/6	Angela continued to make herself available for the team when they had questions to ask, and to provide proactive feedback to the team when needed. She also updated the other stakeholders on the team's progress at their regular monthly meetings.
⊠ Stakeholders **In Agreement** • Stakeholder representatives agree their input is valued and respected by the team • Stakeholder representatives agree with priorities • Stakeholder representatives have agreed on minimal expectations 4/6	By continuously soliciting feedback from the other stakeholders, Angela made sure they still shared the team's objectives and believed in the value of the new system.
⊠ Opportunity **Viable** • A solution has been outlined • Indications are solution can be developed and deployed within constraints • Risks are manageable 4/6	At each iteration, the team inspected and adapted their plans based on their progress and on the feedback they received from Angela and the other stakeholders. By comparing the adapted plans with their understanding of what was happening in the market, Angela and the other stakeholders made sure the opportunity was still viable.

The kernel helps you to remember the importance and impact of the world outside your workplace. By encouraging you to actively keep your eye on these things, the kernel will help you to stay focused on delivering real customer value and, if you do go off track, help you detect it and correct your course.

14.7 EVOLVING A USABLE SYSTEM

Once the architecture was validated (i.e., the skinny system was demonstrated and tested), Smith and his team incrementally added functionality to the system, always ensuring that the system was well tested and potentially shippable (see Table 14-5).

Table 14-5 How the Team Evolved a Usable System

State	How the State Was Achieved
�‑◯ **Software System** **Usable** • System is usable and has desired characteristics • System can be operated by users • Functionality and performance have been tested and accepted • Defect levels acceptable • Release content known 3/6	With the architecture validated, Smith and his team worked to get the requirement items that were demonstrated in the skinny system into a state where they were usable by end users. After that, they started implementing the remaining requirement items in priority order. As they did so, they continually paid close attention to quality, keeping the system usable at all times.
◯ **Requirements** **Acceptable** • Requirements describe a solution acceptable to the stakeholders • The rate of change to agreed-on requirements is low • Value is clear 4/6	Smith had been clarifying the requirements and reviewing them with Angela. After a number of changes, Angela agreed the requirement items were adequate. Both Angela and the team had a clear and agreed-on idea of the scope of the software system.

Table 14-5 How the Team Evolved a Usable System (*continued*)

State	How the State Was Achieved
◻ **Requirements** **Addressed** • Enough requirements are implemented for the system to be acceptable • Stakeholders agree the system is worth making operational 5/6	As the team implemented more and more requirement items, the software system grew to a point where Angela agreed that it could be shipped if necessary. This was a great achievement for the team as, although there were still many more requirements to be implemented, the system was now rich enough in functionality that the company would be happy to release it as version 1 of the new product. The stakeholders wanted more functionality to be added before the scheduled release date, but everyone knew this was "nice to have" and a quality product would be available even if the team failed to add any additional functionality.

What can go wrong here? How can the kernel help you?

The goal here is to produce a software system that the stakeholders agree would be usable in a live environment. This means the software system must have sufficient quality and functionality.

There are two primary ways to get here. The traditional approach is to implement all the required functionality first before verifying the quality. The other approach is to continually ensure quality while functionality (i.e., requirement items) is being incorporated.

The latter approach allows the development team to accept requirement changes more responsively. In addition, the development team is better prepared to release the system at any time since quality is kept stable. It also requires the development team and the stakeholder representatives to work together, agreeing on the requirements to get the system to where it is worth making operational. Sometimes different stakeholder groups bring differing perspectives and even possibly conflicting requirements. The kernel, through its Requirements and Stakeholders alpha checklists, can help the team recognize this situation. While the kernel won't tell you how to solve it, it does remind you of the need to take appropriate action to solve it.

14.8 GETTING TO A GOOD WAY OF WORKING

With the development environment in place, the team collaborating, and the stakeholders in agreement, there was nothing stopping Smith and his team from quickly coming to a point where they worked really well together. The goal was for Smith and his team to be able to run their iterations smoothly, while continuously refining their plans, tuning their way of working, and improving their performance (see Table 14-6).

Table 14-6 How the Team Got to a Good Way of Working

State	How the State Was Achieved
α **Team** **Performing** • Team is working efficiently and effectively • Adapting to changing context • Producing high-quality output • Minimal backtracking and rework • Waste continually eliminated 4/5	At this time, the team members were working well. Whenever there were issues, they stopped their work, came together, and resolved the issue quickly. They were producing high-quality outputs, and they continually adjusted and improved how they did things.
α **Work** **Under Control** • Work going well, risks being managed • Unplanned work and rework under control • Work items completed within estimates • Measures tracked 4/6	The team knew that if they took their eye off the ball things could quickly get out of control. The team continued to make their progress and any impediments they encountered visible to all team members, including Angela. This way, everyone could see that things were heading in the right direction and that the work was still under control.

Table 14-6 How the Team Got to a Good Way of Working (*continued*)

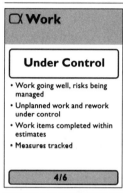

Smith and his team conducted retrospectives at the end of every iteration and began making continuous small improvements to their way of working. As the team members learned more about their development environment and tools, they shared what they had learned and asked their teammates for help when they needed it.

What can go wrong here? How can the kernel help you?

The goal here is to maintain a good way of working throughout development so that the team members can concentrate on building good software.

What happens if the way of working is not working well? It depends on the degree of difficulties faced. In the best case, it might be just frustration, producing some waste, or accumulating some (small) technical debt, which may not be really delaying the product or resulting in reduced quality in the eyes of the stakeholders. In short, the team could live with this. In the worst case, it might cause fights, delays, and unacceptable quality. The remedy is to work iteratively. Each iteration exercises the way of working and highlights what isn't working well through the alphas. The kernel alpha states and their checklists make what your team is doing more tangible, helping you to quickly pinpoint and solve problems.

14.9 EVOLVING A DEPLOYABLE SOLUTION— CONCLUDING THE WORK

Although the system was potentially releasable, the team still had more work to do to get it ready. They needed to hand the product over to production and make sure the initial release was synchronized with the company's marketing plans. They also had to deal with the desires of their stakeholders, who wanted the initial release to be feature-rich and go well beyond the minimal functionality needed by a usable system.

The team agreed to use their remaining two iterations to continue adding functionality to the system, while concluding the work that was needed in order to get the system accepted and ready to hand over to production.

The goal was to get the system ready and accepted so that they could pass the Decision to Go Live milestone. This, their final development milestone, is summarized in Figure 14-4.

- In the Customer area of concern it was all about making sure the stakeholders were satisfied that the system could be deployed, and that the opportunity had been successfully addressed.

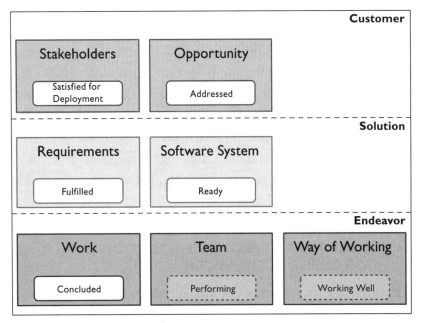

Figure 14-4 The final development milestone

- In the Solution area of concern it was all about evolving the system so that it fulfilled the requirements while making sure the software system was ready for transition to production and operational use.

- In the Endeavor area of concern it was all about concluding the development work while making sure the team continued to perform and the way of working continued to work well.

14.10 GAINING ACCEPTANCE

Angela watched the development closely to determine if the software system had come to a point where it would satisfy the stakeholders and address the opportunity. When the software system was ready, Angela and the development team worked together to achieve acceptance, an important part of the Decision to Go Live milestone. No software could be released unless the stakeholders formally accepted it (see Table 14-7).

Table 14-7 How the Team Gained Acceptance

State	How the State Was Achieved
◯ Stakeholders **Satisfied for Deployment** • Stakeholder representatives provide feedback on system from their stakeholder group perspective • Stakeholder representatives confirm system is ready for deployment 5/6	Angela worked with the other stakeholders to nail down the criteria for deployment and provided the feedback on the system to the team. Smith and his team made the finishing touches to the software system. After a successful acceptance test, the stakeholders were satisfied that the system could be deployed.

continues

Table 14-7 How the Team Gained Acceptance (*continued*)

State	How the State Was Achieved
◯ Opportunity **Addressed** • A solution has been produced that demonstrably addresses opportunity • A usable system is available • Stakeholders agree the system is worth deploying • Stakeholders are satisfied the solution addresses the opportunity 5/6	Following the final acceptance testing everyone agreed that Angela's initial idea was now realized. The system was ready to be launched.

What can go wrong here? How can the kernel help you?

Sometimes stakeholder representatives don't adequately communicate the needs of the group they represent. When stakeholder representatives fail to live up to their responsibilities in a timely way they put the success of the software endeavor at risk. The kernel helps to keep the importance of these responsibilities visible to both the team and its stakeholders.

14.11 GETTING TO DELIVERY

Smith and his team incrementally added functionality to the system until a point when Angela deemed that requirements had been fulfilled and the system was ready for acceptance testing.

The team also addressed the final pieces of documentation needed to support the handover to production, and carried out the final performance and security checks needed to demonstrate that the system was ready to go live.

After a successful acceptance test, the system was made available to its users (see Table 14-8).

Table 14-8 How the Team Got to Delivery

State	How the State Was Achieved
◻ **Requirements** **Fulfilled** • The system fully satisfies the requirements and the need • There are no outstanding requirement items preventing completion 6/6	Smith and his team incrementally implemented the requirement items into the software system, fixing critical defects as they were found. After running through acceptance tests, Angela and the other stakeholders agreed that the requirements were fulfilled.
◻ **Software System** **Ready** • User documentation available • Stakeholder representatives accept system • Stakeholder representatives want to make system operational 4/6	In parallel with the acceptance testing the team conducted a dress rehearsal of the go-live for the system with their colleagues in production, and ran the final performance and security tests in the company's internal production environment. Smith prepared the release notes. Dick and Harriet prepared the application user guide. The system was now ready.

What can go wrong here? How can the kernel help you?

The goal here was to bring the development work to a conclusion and achieve final acceptance from the stakeholders. If you follow the advice of the kernel, you will have regular contact with the stakeholder representatives, and a software system that is demonstrated to be architecturally stable, usable, functionally satisfactory, and potentially shippable. If the system you are developing gets rejected at this point, you have most likely missed something important in your evaluation of the alpha states.

Here are a few questions you could ask yourself to determine what went wrong, and what needs to be done to get back on course.

- Were all of the stakeholder representatives really involved, and did they really reach agreement?
- Did the stakeholders accept the system as ready for deployment, and agree that it met the requirements?
- Did the stakeholders accept that the requirements reflect what the system actually does?

These are just a few of the questions you could ask to help isolate the root cause. Once the root cause is isolated the next step is to identify the proper course of action to resolve the issue. Just as the kernel helped us identify where we were and where we needed to go next, it can also be used to troubleshoot a problem and get your software endeavor back on track.

For example, sometimes management or the team wants to ship too early. In such situations someone needs to explain the potential consequences dissatisfied customers can have on future business. The Software System: Ready, Requirements: Fulfilled, and Stakeholders: Satisfied for Deployment checklists can remind the team and its management that all stakeholder groups need to agree that the system is ready for operational use.

14.12 DONE! COMPLETING DEVELOPMENT WORK

The project is entering its final two iterations. It is essential that the team makes sure they have concluded their work and are ready to hand everything over to the production team for deployment, support, and maintenance (see Table 14-9).

The team also needed to keep an eye on its own performance and way of working (see Table 14-10).

Table 14-9 How the Team Completed Development Work

State	How the State Was Achieved
⊠ Work **Concluded** • Work to produce results has been finished • Work results are being achieved • The client has accepted the resultant software system 5/6	The team made the final revisions to their plans, making sure they had recorded their lessons learned and kept everything up to date. The system, its documentation, the way of working, and so forth were all handed over to the production team.

Table 14-10 How the Team Kept an Eye on Its Own Performance

State	How the State Was Maintained
⊠ Team **Performing** • Team is working efficiently and effectively • Adapting to changing context • Producing high-quality output • Minimal backtracking and rework • Waste continually eliminated 4/5	The team continued producing high-quality outputs, and adjusting and improving how they do things.
⊠ Way of Working **Working Well** • Way of working is working well for team • Team members are making progress as planned • Team naturally applies practices without thinking about them • Tools naturally support way of working 5/6	The team continued holding retrospectives at the end of every iteration, and making continuous small improvements to their way of working. They also shared their way of working with their colleagues in production to help them get ready to take over the support and maintenance of the system.

What can go wrong here? How can the kernel help you?

The goal here is to bring the work to a successful conclusion while maintaining the enthusiasm and performance of the team. The alphas and their states can help you to make sure everything is wrapped up properly and that a healthy system is handed over for support and maintenance.

14.13 HOW THE KERNEL HELPS YOU DEVELOP GREAT SOFTWARE

This chapter showed you how the kernel can help you when you are developing software by walking through many of the alphas and their states. We focused on the usefulness of the kernel, which includes several aspects.

- It defines intermediate points to help a team focus on their immediate next step.

- It considers the different dimensions of software development so that the development team can address all dimensions in a balanced manner.

- It allows you to choose how to achieve the states. This gives you flexibility in how to deal with your situation.

The alphas and the states are reminders to help you achieve your goal without missing anything essential, reminders that don't require that you follow any specific methodology or life cycle.

15

Operating the Software

In this chapter we will walk through the last few states in the kernel, looking at how the production team used the kernel to help with the deployment, support, and maintenance of the application.

15.1 SETTING THE SCENE

When the system was handed over from the development team to production, the production team received the following evidence.

- The stakeholders were satisfied for deployment.
- The opportunity had been addressed.
- The requirements had been fulfilled.
- The software system was ready.

They also knew the development team was still available to support the application, as the work had not yet been closed nor the team adjourned.

The production team was a specialist team led by Jones. This team was responsible for (1) deploying all the software systems produced by Smith's department, and (2) providing first-line support and maintenance on the products deployed.

The maintenance was limited to emergency bug fixes and configuration changes. All enhancement requests, even the smallest ones, were batched up and handled as new development work by Smith's department.

Jones's team didn't wait for the new software system to be delivered before they started work. They had already been involved in the development work, before the official handover, helping with the dress rehearsals and learning about the new application. In terms of the kernel, the state of their endeavor could be summed up as shown in Figure 15-1.

Once the development team was sure they would be able to deliver a timely release the production work was initiated. The production team was already in place, supporting the other applications produced by Smith's department. The plans for the use and distribution of the new application showed that the existing team would be able to cope with the increased work, so there was no need to form a new team. By working with the development team, contributing to the acceptance testing and, in particular, the dress rehearsals, the production team was able to make sure the deployment, maintenance, and support work was properly prepared.

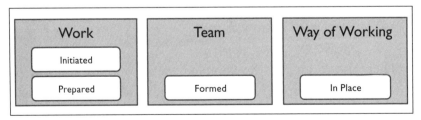

Figure 15-1 The state of the production endeavor

Jones's team already had their support and deployment practices in place. Smith's team also handed over the development way of working to help them with any maintenance they might have to do. As Jones's team was experienced and received a proper handover from Smith's team, they were confident that the way of working was already in place.

The work of Jones's team always followed the same pattern.

1. Successfully deploy the system.

2. Support the system until retirement.

Their first objective was to achieve the Successfully Deployed milestone. This meant making the new software system operational, making sure the stakeholders were satisfied in its use and that benefit was being accrued, and making sure that any emergency changes that were made didn't result in the requirements no longer being fulfilled.

Figure 15-2 shows the Successfully Deployed milestone using the alphas from the Customer and Solution areas of concern.

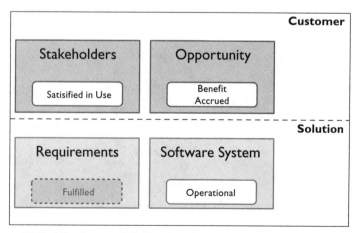

Figure 15-2   The Successfully Deployed milestone

The overall objective of Jones's team was to support the system until it was retired, either because the application was no longer needed or because it was replaced by a new version provided by Smith's department.

This meant making sure the stakeholders were still satisfied in their use of the system and that the use of the system was still accruing benefit for the users and the company. They also needed to make sure the system was kept operational and fulfilling the initial requirements.

In terms of the kernel, the team's long-term responsibilities with regard to the customers and the solution are summed up in Figure 15-3.

The situation regarding the Endeavor area of concern was a little more complicated as now there were two distinct teams and two distinct pieces of work. We will look at this in more detail when we look at what the teams did to (1) successfully deploy the system, and (2) support the application until its retirement.

Again we will look at what was done in each area of concern to achieve each of these milestones.

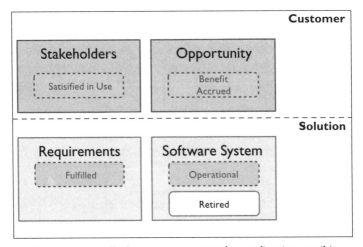

Figure 15-3 The overall objective: support the application until its retirement

15.2 GOING LIVE—SUCCESSFULLY DEPLOYING THE SYSTEM

The teams had already agreed on the release date for the new application with the stakeholders, and that there would be a four-week warranty period while the early adopters provided feedback and started to receive benefit from the purchase and use of the new application. It was agreed that if all went well Smith's team would be able to stand down and close the development work, with Jones's team taking on full responsibility for the application.

The goal of the two teams was to achieve the Successfully Deployed milestone, which is summarized in Figure 15-4.

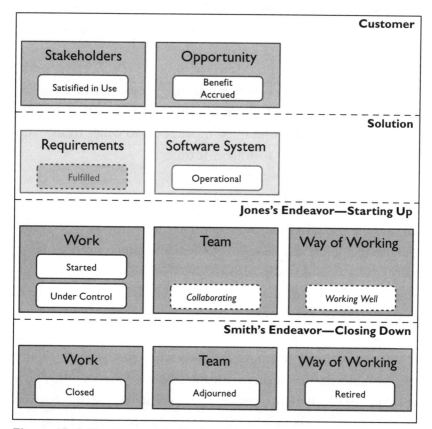

Figure 15-4 The Successfully Deployed milestone

- In the Customer area of concern it was all about gaining feedback from the actual use of the system to make sure the stakeholders were satisfied in the use of the new application, and to see benefit being accrued from the investment in addressing the opportunity.

- In the Solution area of concern it was all about making the software system operational and checking that the requirements were fulfilled in the operational environment.

- In the Endeavor area of concern we have the beginning of Jones's support and maintenance endeavor where the work needs to be started and brought under control. Although not essential, it is also hoped that the team will be successfully collaborating and that the way of working will be working well by the time the deployment is completed.

We also have the closing down of Smith's development work, which, once the system is successfully in operation, will be closed and the team adjourned. From Smith's perspective they will be retiring their way of working by moving on to other things and handing the work over to Jones's team.

15.3 DEPLOYING THE SYSTEM

Deploying the system is about more than just making the software available for use. Support and maintenance need to be in place, the stakeholders must be happy with the deployment, and emergency fixes may be required to correct any serious problems found by the early adopters.

Table 15-1 shows how Jones's and Smith's teams worked together to achieve this. (As with the tables in Chapters 13 and 14, the tables in this chapter are formatted into two columns, with the column on the left showing the alpha states and the column on the right describing what the team did to achieve the state.)

Table 15-1 How the Team Deployed the System

State	How the State Was Achieved
☐ **Software System** **Operational** • System in use in operational environment • System available to intended users • At least one example of system is fully operational • System supported to agreed-on service levels 5/6	After the successful acceptance of the system, Smith and Jones worked together to get the application available both pre-installed on the company's phones and on the application market (i.e., the likes of the Android Market and Apple App Store). Jones and her team added the new application to those supported by their help desk, and started to track usage and problem reports. To check the availability Angela downloaded the application from the application market and started using it. There were some teething problems on a number of old models of the company's phones, which led to a number of emergency fixes being produced and software updates distributed. The two teams worked together to address these problems and update the operational system.
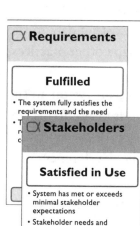 ☐ **Requirements** **Fulfilled** • The system fully satisfies the requirements and the need ☐ **Stakeholders** **Satisfied in Use** • System has met or exceeds minimal stakeholder expectations • Stakeholder needs and expectations are being met 6/6	The feedback from the early adopters was generally very favorable with no other problems reported and high satisfaction ratings being recorded on the reviews submitted to the app stores. This, combined with additional feedback from the stakeholders, was enough to show that the stakeholders were satisfied in the use of the new application and that the requirements were fulfilled just as well in the operational environment as they were in the test environments.

continues

Table 15-1 How the Team Deployed the System (*continued*)

State	How the State Was Achieved
◻ Opportunity **Benefit Accrued** • Operational use creating tangible benefits • Return on investment profile at least as good as anticipated 6/6	Revenue was being collected from downloads of the application, and sales of the new phones were going well. The application was so successful that the company started to feature it explicitly in the advertisements for its phones.

What can go wrong here? How can the kernel help you?

Delivering the system can present a whole range of challenges depending on the kind of development you are doing. For example, if you are building some custom enterprise application, this would mean conducting training, migrating existing data to the new system, and so on. This would require many other practices, which can be defined on top of the kernel.

The kernel helps us by reminding us to keep an eye on all the aspects of the endeavor. For example, it reminds us not to declare victory before we have satisfied the actual users of the system or provided any benefit to those who funded the development.

15.4 HANDING OVER BETWEEN THE TWO TEAMS

As well as successfully deploying the system, Smith and Jones needed to complete the handover between the two teams.

Let's look at how Jones's team got started (see Table 15-2).

In parallel with the ramp-up of Jones's team, Smith's team was getting to the end of their work. Let's look at how they closed out their work (see Table 15-3).

Table 15-2 How the Team Completed the Handover

State	How the State Was Achieved
ɑ Work **Started** • Development work has started • Work progress is monitored • Work is broken down into actionable items with clear definition of done • Team members are accepting and progress work items 3/6	Jones's team accepted the ready-to-deploy application from Smith's team, and added the application to their list of supported applications. This was all that was needed to start the work.
ɑ Work **Under Control** • Work going well, risks being managed • Unplanned work and rework under control • Work items completed within estimates • Measures tracked 4/6	After the first month it was clear that the application was working well, emergency fixes could be generated when needed, and the support team could handle the queries from the application's users. The team and their stakeholders agreed that they had the work under control.
ɑ Team **Collaborating** • Members working as one unit • Communication is open and honest • Members focused on team mission • Success of team ahead of personal objectives 3/5	Jones's team found the application well documented and easy to support. The lack of any real teething problems meant the team was quickly working well together, and helping one another when and where needed.

continues

Table 15-2 How the Team Completed the Handover (*continued*)

State	How the State Was Achieved
☒ **Way of Working** **Working Well** • Way of working is working well for team • Team members are making progress as planned • Team naturally applies practices without thinking about them • Tools naturally support way of working 5/6	After the handover from Smith the team found that they had all the tools they needed to maintain the application, and after making the first few emergency changes they agreed that it was working well.

Table 15-3 How the Team Closed Out Their Work

State	How the State Was Achieved
☒ **Work** **Closed** • All remaining housekeeping tasks completed, and work offically closed • Everything has been archived • Lessons learned and metrics made available 6/6	With the successful deployment of the application and the handover to Jones's team. the work for Smith's team was over. They had a final meeting with all their stakeholders where Dave organized some champagne to celebrate the success of the new product, and Angela told everybody about her latest idea.
☒ **Team** **Adjourned** • Team no longer accountable • Responsibilities handed over • Members available for other assignments 5/5	With the closure of the work on this application, Dave reassigned the team to work on a different application. Although the team stayed together, as far as this endeavor was concerned they were stood down and were no longer available for work on the application.

Table 15-3 How the Team Closed Out Their Work (*continued*)

State	How the State Was Achieved
☐ **Way of Working** **Retired** • Way of working is no longer in use by team • Lessons learned are shared for future use 6/6	With the conclusion of the work, the team did a final retrospective and shared their lessons learned with Jones's team, who now owned the way of working.

What can go wrong here? How can the kernel help you?

It's amazing how often development teams, even iterative ones, think that their work is over once they hand the software over to the maintenance and support teams. Having worked collaboratively to develop the software they think they can adopt a fire-and-forget attitude to their colleagues in operations and support. The kernel reminds you of the importance of seeing your development through to the end, and helps you to understand the state of your work and team, as well as that of your colleagues.

15.5 SUPPORTING THE SYSTEM UNTIL RETIREMENT

Now that Smith's team had been adjourned from the work, Jones and her team had full ownership of the application, which they would maintain until the application was retired. Their overall objective is summarized in terms of alpha states in Figure 15-5.

- In the Customer area of concern the team had to keep an eye on the level of customer satisfaction and the amount of benefit being accrued. This would help the stakeholders to decide whether to continue supporting the application.

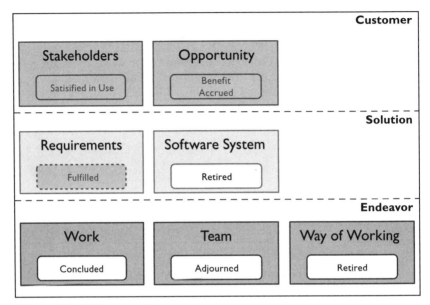

Figure 15-5 The end of the road

- In the Solution area of concern the team had to continue their support until the application was retired.

- In the Endeavor area of concern they had to keep an eye on the state of their work, the team, and their way of working. Eventually the work would be concluded, the team adjourned, and the way of working retired.

Let's take a brief look at how Jones and her team achieved their objectives during this potentially long period of support and maintenance (see Table 15-4).

What can go wrong here? How can the kernel help you?

Lots of things can go wrong once an application is live. Regardless of what happens, the alpha states and their checklists can help you understand your responsibilities and whether the application has regressed to an earlier state.

Table 15-4 How the Team Supported the System until Retirement

State	How the State Was Achieved
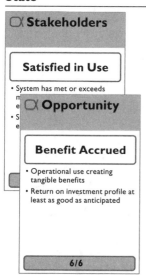	The team collected a number of measures around the usage of the application, the number of downloads, the revenue generated, and customer satisfaction. Once a month these were shared with the stakeholders.
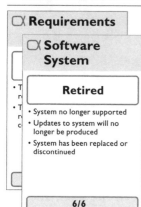	The application was very successful and customer feedback generated lots of suggestions for improvements and extensions to the application. The stakeholders agreed to invest in a second release of the software to again be developed by Dave, Smith and his team, and Angela. Jones's team therefore had to continue support of release 1 until the new release could be deployed and support for release 1 could be discontinued. Plans were put in place to end-of-life release 1 and withdraw support two months after the successful deployment of release 2. In this way, Jones and her team retired the original application.

continues

Table 15-4 How the Team Supported the System until Retirement (*continued*)

State	How the State Was Achieved
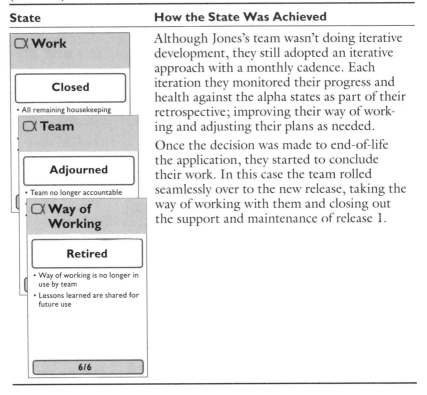	Although Jones's team wasn't doing iterative development, they still adopted an iterative approach with a monthly cadence. Each iteration they monitored their progress and health against the alpha states as part of their retrospective; improving their way of working and adjusting their plans as needed. Once the decision was made to end-of-life the application, they started to conclude their work. In this case the team rolled seamlessly over to the new release, taking the way of working with them and closing out the support and maintenance of release 1.

15.6 OUR STORY ENDS

This is where we leave our story. The application has been successfully developed and deployed and is now in the safe hands of Jones and her team. We have seen the states of all kernel alphas and how they can help teams develop, deploy, and support their applications.

In the next part of the book we will look at how the kernel can be scaled to help address larger and more complex situations.

FURTHER READING

Boehm, B., and R. Turner. 2003. *Balancing Agility and Discipline: A Guide for the Perplexed* (Boston: Addison-Wesley).

Leffingwell, D. 2011. *Agile Software Requirements: Lean Requirements Practices for Teams, Programs, and the Enterprise.* Agile Software Development Series (Boston: Addison-Wesley).

Ambler, S.W., and M. Lines. 2012. *Disciplined Agile Delivery: A Practitioner's Guide to Agile Software Delivery in the Enterprise* (Boston: IBM Press).

Jacobson, I., I. Spence, and K. Bittner. *Use-Case 2.0* (Ivar Jacobson International, ebook).

PART IV

SCALING DEVELOPMENT WITH THE KERNEL

We showed in Parts II and III how a small team can use the kernel to drive software development. We assumed the team members are competent and can determine what to do by referring to the alpha state criteria.

Will this work for all kinds of development, big or small, collocated or distributed teams, in-house or outsourced? In short, does the kernel scale?

This part of the book will discuss different dimensions of scaling and how practices on top of the kernel can help you address the challenges of more complex and large development.

16

What Does It Mean to Scale?

The term *scale* can connote different ideas. In this chapter we clarify what we mean by "scaling" and how the kernel approach helps scaling. The kernel contains the essential elements of software engineering, but does not contain everything a team needs to know or do in specific situations. It is a good starting point to scale to any kind of software development endeavor, including those with a large number of participants.

If you are involved in a large development, you are likely to face at least three major challenges.

1. All team members may not possess the needed competencies. Some may need more explicit guidance beyond what the kernel provides.

2. Different kinds of software endeavors have different risks and constraints, and therefore face different challenges. What is the most appropriate approach to run development?

3. With large development, coordination of the work among members becomes a challenge. How do you ensure that members discuss, share, and agree on their plans, their progress, and the results of their work?

These are three distinct challenges to scaling. Accordingly, when considering what it means to scale we need to address three corresponding dimensions of scaling (see Figure 16-1), all of which may happen at the same time in specific situations.

- *Zooming in:* We call the first dimension "zooming in," and it is about providing guidance beyond what the kernel provides. This is necessary in several cases. First, inexperienced members need more guidance. Second, larger teams with members having different backgrounds need further details to ensure that they have a common understanding of how to conduct development. This additional guidance comes in the form of what SEMAT refers to as *practices*, which are extensions to the kernel. SEMAT provides a way to describe and assemble practices together in a systematic manner. For team members it is a practical way to understand how to apply practices, and how different practices work together.

- *Reaching out:* The second dimension is "reaching out," and it is about extending the kernel with appropriate practices to

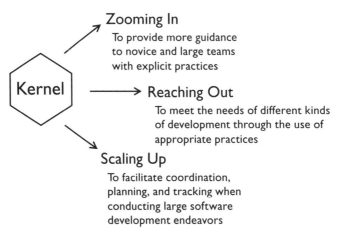

Figure 16-1 Dimensions of scaling

meet the specific needs of different kinds of development. Every development endeavor is different. In-house development is different from outsourced or offshore development. Web development is different from embedded development, and so on. Each development endeavor has its own set of challenges, and consequently requires its own set of practices.

Reaching out is about selecting appropriate practices and building the right *method* (which is a composition of practices on top of the kernel) to address the risks and challenges for a particular software endeavor. A simple approach to practices empowers a team to build their own method. This begins with the kernel, on top of which the team selects appropriate practices to form its own method. Large organizations usually have several prebuilt methods for teams to choose from. Thus, they have a prebuilt method for in-house development, a prebuilt method for offshore development, and so on. Each prebuilt method comprises mandatory practices on top of the kernel so that teams have more guidance to start beyond the kernel. Teams are still permitted to add additional practices as needed.

- *Scaling up:* We call the third dimension "scaling up," and it is about expanding the use of the kernel from a team with a small number of members and low complexity to endeavors involving large numbers of people and systems with high complexity. Scaling up happens in large development, such as enterprise systems, product lines, and so on. These systems are usually complex, developed in a distributed manner at multiple sites, or even outsourced. They typically involve many different frameworks and technologies. Here we often are no longer dealing with a single set of requirements, a single software system, and a single team, but multiple sets of requirements, multiple software systems (subsystems), and multiple teams. In such situations, it is important to have a good way to organize work and teams, to visualize progress, and to coordinate work among teams.

In these more complex cases, it is important to provide tools and mechanisms for teams to self-manage. The kernel, with its alphas, provides the tools for team members to design the way teams collaborate with other teams and members collaborate with other members. Traditional approaches to scaling often rely on strengthening the command hierarchy and adding more checks, which can lead to bottlenecks and unnecessary conflicts. Modern approaches emphasize self-management, self-organization, and even self-governance. In this part of the book we will demonstrate, with examples using the aforementioned three dimensions of scaling, how the kernel approach scales.

17

Zooming In to Provide Details

The kernel does not attempt to provide all possible guidance to teams—just the essence. Thus, for inexperienced team members, further guidance is needed. Zooming in is about providing the details that inexperienced team members might need. Zooming in is also necessary in larger organizations where team members, more often than not, have different backgrounds and experiences. In such cases, team members, even though they have experience, need further details to ensure that they have a common understanding of how they should conduct development.

We want to emphasize the importance of not providing guidance about everything, but to focus on what inexperienced team members have difficulty with. This is an important difference compared to traditional approaches that describe everything team members may possibly need, which results in heavyweight descriptions. The kernel approach supports this through precise and selectable practices that address specific challenges.

Definition

A practice provides guidance to deal with some dimension of software development.

179

For example, if a team has challenges with eliciting requirements, they need a requirements elicitation practice; if a team has challenges with conducting an acceptance test, they need an acceptance testing practice, and so on.

In addition to understanding how to use individual practices, team members need to understand how a set of practices are used together, because they need to address multiple challenges simultaneously (e.g., both requirements elicitation and acceptance testing).

17.1 MAKING PRACTICES PRECISE FOR INEXPERIENCED MEMBERS

The problem today is that although *practice* is a commonly used term in the software development industry, it is, at best, loosely defined. Different people have different ideas of what a practice is, and they use different ways to describe a particular practice. Thus, inexperienced team members can find it hard to understand how a practice is supposed to work, and how multiple practices are supposed to work together. This is especially true when practices come from different sources. More importantly, without understanding how practices are supposed to work together, teams often degenerate into individuals or smaller groups working alone (i.e., one group of people doing requirements, and another group working on testing, and not collaborating well).

The kernel provides a simple language,[1] which we will henceforth call the kernel language, to address these problems by providing a precise way to describe practices. The kernel language does so in a manner that is easy for inexperienced members to apply in terms of the things to work with, and the things to do when using a practice. The things to work with comprise alphas, which are the main emphasis in this book, and also *work*

---

1. For more details on the kernel language, please refer to the SEMAT submission.

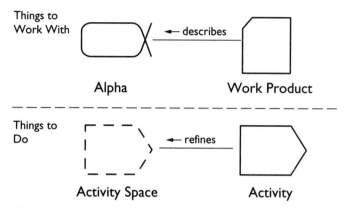

Figure 17-1 Glimpse of the kernel language

products (see Figure 17-1). Work products are physical documents, or reports, that the team produces as evidence when they progress alphas.

The things to do comprise activity spaces, which we introduced in Chapter 3, and activities, which provide more detailed guidance on how to achieve alpha states.

In addition, the kernel language provides a way to understand how practices work together through what is known as *practice composition*. Basically, practice composition is about merging two separate practices to become a bigger practice.

For illustrative purposes, we will consider two practices in this chapter, namely:

1. A requirements elicitation practice

2. An acceptance testing practice

We chose these two practices because they overlap, and through them we can demonstrate how the kernel language provides a systematic way to describe and compose practices and thereby helps teams understand how separate practices can work together.

17.2 AN EXAMPLE: A REQUIREMENTS ELICITATION PRACTICE

Our first example is a requirements elicitation practice. Its purpose is to ensure that the team is developing something of value to customers with the agreement from stakeholders.

We describe how to apply this practice in terms of the things to work with and the things to do (see Figure 17-2).

- *Thing to work with:* This practice provides guidance to clarify the opportunity with stakeholders to gain a correct understanding of requirements. Requirements are captured in a work product known as a Feature List. This is visually depicted in Figure 17-2 where the Feature List is attached to the Requirements alpha.

- *Things to do:* This practice provides guidance on how to conduct several activities, namely:

  1. Agree on what is of value to users to explore possibilities

  2. Walk through the usage of the system to understand requirements

  3. Conduct user demos as a way to involve stakeholders

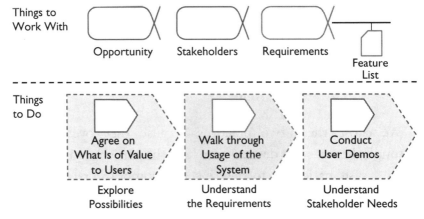

Figure 17-2 A requirements elicitation practice

- *Using the practice:* Using the requirements elicitation practice follows the approach we discussed earlier in the book. A team determines its current state of development, and in this case the emphasis is on the Opportunity, Stakeholders, and Requirements alphas as highlighted in the Things to Work With section of Figure 17-2. The practice provides guidance through activities describing how to progress to the next state. For brevity, we will consider just the Requirements alpha (see Figure 17-3). These activities can be conducted iteratively over a number of iterations.

Figure 17-3 shows the mapping from Requirements alpha states to activities. It guides team members in what to do when they want to achieve a particular Requirements alpha state. For example, the practice recommends conducting the activity Agree on What Is of Value to Users (through requirements brainstorming and prioritization) to achieve the Requirements Conceived and Bounded states.

Note that behind each activity or work product icon is a set of guidelines to conduct the activity or work on the work product. These guidelines can be as light or as detailed as needed in the situation. Just like there are cards for alphas, there can be cards for work products. Just as we can condense the kernel into a deck of cards, we can also present each practice as a set of cards.

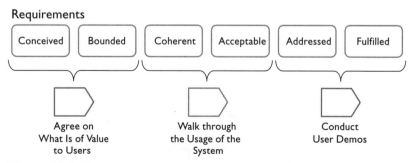

Figure 17-3 Using the requirements elicitation practice

Activities and Their Contribution to Alpha State Progression

The ultimate objective of conducting an activity is to help produce high-quality software. Alpha target states have associated critical activities needed to achieve the objective. A single activity can progress an alpha through more than one state. Using the preceding example, if the endeavor is not complex or if there is sufficient stakeholder participation, a single execution of the activity Agree on What Is of Value to Users can progress the Requirements alpha to the Bounded state. However, if the stakeholders cannot reach agreement as to the scope of the requirements, they can conduct the same activity again, but with a slightly different emphasis to reach the Bounded state.

17.3 AN EXAMPLE: AN ACCEPTANCE TESTING PRACTICE

Our next example is an acceptance testing practice. Its purpose is to agree on the acceptance test cases early during development and use them to drive development work. Figure 17-4 depicts the elements of this practice.

As before, we describe the acceptance testing practice by considering the things to work with and the things to do.

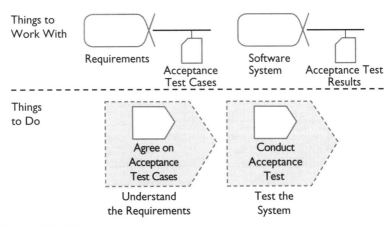

Figure 17-4 An acceptance testing practice

- *Things to work with:* The acceptance testing practice focuses on the Requirements and Software System alphas. It provides guidance in how to clarify requirements by agreeing on Acceptance Test Cases, and subsequently evaluate the quality of the system by reviewing the Acceptance Test Results.

- *Things to do:* The acceptance testing practice provides guidance on how to conduct activities, namely:

  1. Agree on acceptance test cases as a way to understand the requirements

  2. Conduct an acceptance test to test the system

- *Using the practice:* Using the acceptance testing practice follows the same approach of determining current states and agreeing on what to do to progress to the next state. This is shown in Figure 17-5 for the Requirements alpha. Again, the activities can be conducted iteratively.

  1. This practice assumes that the team has already bounded their requirements.

  2. This practice provides guidance in how to agree on acceptance test cases to achieve the Requirements Coherent and Acceptable states.

  3. This practice also provides guidance as to how to conduct an acceptance test to achieve the Addressed and Fulfilled states.

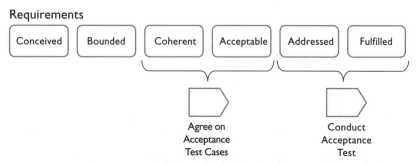

Figure 17-5 Using the acceptance testing practice

17.4 UNDERSTANDING HOW PRACTICES WORK TOGETHER

A team member who is applying the requirements elicitation and acceptance testing practices needs to compose them together. By providing a clear and systematic way to describe practices, as we have shown in this chapter, this composition becomes simple. Basically, we consider practice composition in terms of the following:

1. Composing the things to work with

2. Composing the things to do

3. Using the composed practices

- *Composing the things to work with:* Figure 17-6 shows the composition of the things to work with. Composition is just simply merging. This is why all the things to work with in both practices appear in Figure 17-6. The overlap between the two practices can be seen through the Requirements alpha, which has two work products: Feature List and Acceptance Test Cases. *Overlap* means the persons who are responsible for each work product must work together and make sure these work products are consistent. In this case the Feature List and the Acceptance Test Cases must be consistent.

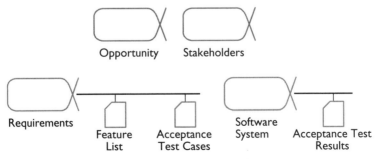

Figure 17-6 Composing the things to work with

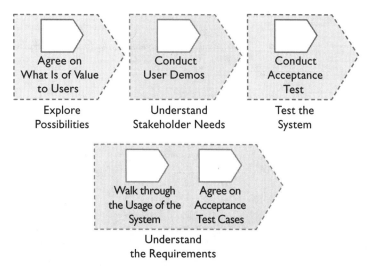

Figure 17-7 Composing the things to do

- *Composing the things to do:* Figure 17-7 shows the composition of the things to do; all elements that exist in the individual practices also appear in the composition. The overlap is evident in the Understand the Requirements activity space, which has activities from the respective practices. This indicates *one* of the following.

  1. The two activities, where possible, should be conducted together.

  2. The results of the two activities must be consistent.

- *Using the composed practices:* When using the composed practices a team needs to consider all the alphas involved. For illustrative purposes, Figure 17-8 shows how a team would progress the Requirements alpha. To achieve the initial two states, the team would conduct the activity Agree on What Is of Value to Users. To achieve the Requirements Coherent and Acceptable states, the composed practices suggest the team both Walk through the Usage of the System

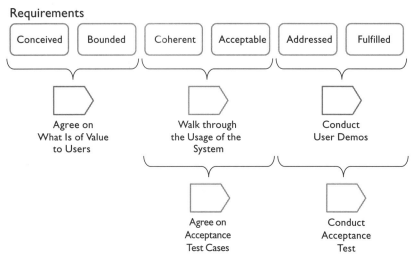

Requirements

Figure 17-8 Using the composed practices

and Agree on Acceptance Test Cases. For teams that have clear roles and responsibilities between requirements and testing (as in the case of more traditional organizations), it provides guidance as to how members can break down the barriers and collaborate better.

17.5 VALUE OF PRECISE PRACTICES

In this chapter we demonstrated that both individual practices (requirements elicitation and acceptance testing) are described and used in much the same way as their composition. We describe them in terms of things to work with and things to do, and we use them by progressing alpha states based on recommended activities. SEMAT gives a precise meaning to the term *practices:* It provides a simple language to describe practices (in terms of things to work with [alphas and work products] and things to do [activity spaces and activities]), first using elements from the kernel and then attaching other elements where required. Beginning from the kernel is important, because the kernel is the foundation; it provides a common terminology and a simple way through alpha states to progress development. In addition, a systematic way to describe practices leads to a systematic and simple way to compose practices. To practitioners, especially inexperienced practitioners, it becomes easier to learn how different practices work together and to apply them.

18

Reaching Out to Different Kinds of Development

Different development endeavors (such as in-house development, offshore development, custom development, product development, etc.) face different risks and challenges, and therefore need different sets of practices. Reaching out is about choosing an appropriate set of practices for a development team. A method is a composition of such a set of practices.

Definition

A method is a composition of practices.

Because methods directly affect how a team does its work, we want to empower teams to understand how to build their own method, rather than forcing a method onto the team. To understand how the selected practices work together, it is necessary to describe them in a common and composable manner, and we demonstrated that in Chapter 17.

With the kernel approach, building a method is simple. A team can start with the practices they need and gradually evolve its method as development progresses. For larger organizations, it is often useful to provide a predefined method that comprises the kernel and several mandated practices, on top of which the team can add other practices to adapt it to their specific needs.

18.1 AGREEING ON THE PRACTICES TO USE

To collaborate effectively the members of a team have to agree on which practices to use. This set of practices defines how the team will conduct their software development and forms their method.

A team may select the practices they are familiar with and believe will help them the most. In most cases, the following occurs. A team usually has something it likes from its existing method and something it wants to remove and replace with something better. So the team starts with the kernel and selects and composes practices to form a method that consists only of what the team wants to keep from its existing method and the new practices it wants to adopt to form its own method.

As an example, Figure 18-1 shows Smith's team's method, which is composed of the requirements elicitation practice, acceptance testing practice, and practices from various other sources. The practices the team selects may be ones that it devises, or ones that it borrows from industry, such as user stories, use cases or test-driven development.

Figure 18-1 Building your own method by selecting the practices you need

18.2 ADAPTING TO YOUR DEVELOPMENT LIFE CYCLE

When it comes to building a method, it is important to start with the big picture. Typically, teams consider their development life cycle because it lays the overall strategy to deliver the software system to the customer community. A life cycle defines a set of milestones that serves as a guide for a team to make its development plans, and for the larger organization to make its resource, and even funding, plans. Different kinds of software endeavors have different risks and constraints, and need different life cycles. There is no one-size-fits-all solution. For simplicity, let's assume that a development life cycle has three major phases.

1. *Pre-development:* This is before any actual development (requirements design, coding, and testing) starts, and comprises preparatory work.

2. *Development:* This is when the team development occurs, and it consists of requirements design, coding, and testing.

3. *Post-development:* This is when the software system is available to end users.

Different life cycles differ from one another by how the business makes a decision to exit one phase and proceed to the next. A high-ceremony organization may prefer more up-front investigation before proceeding with development, whereas a low-ceremony organization may prefer to start development straight away. Either way, the kernel provides a way to build your own development life cycle by associating alpha states to the life-cycle phases. Figures 18-2 and 18-3 give two examples of development life cycles. The labels 1 through 6 indicate the states of the respective alphas.

The key differences between Figures 18-2 (modern development life cycle) and 18-3 (waterfall development life cycle) are the

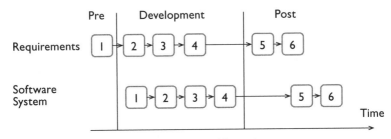

Figure 18-2 The modern development life cycle

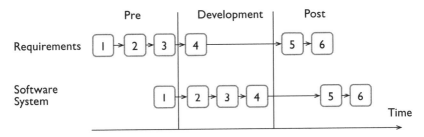

Figure 18-3 The waterfall development life cycle

allocation of states between the pre-development phase and the development phase. The modern approach starts development earlier. As you can see we have just used the same alpha states to describe both the traditional waterfall and modern development life cycles. This is very useful because it means practices can be described independently of the life cycle.[1]

18.3 BUILDING A METHOD INCREMENTALLY DURING DEVELOPMENT

Building a method for your team is not something you need to complete up front before any work starts (i.e., you do not need to select all the practices you need up front). You can adopt a just-in-time approach, or more accurately, a little ahead of time.

---

1. It is worth noting that most projects do not just choose between these two simple cases. In reality there are degrees of how much up-front work is needed.

As we mentioned in Part II of the book, development involves a number of Plan-Do-Check-Adapt cycles. With the kernel approach, you determine the current alpha states and plan how to achieve the next states. Practices provide additional guidance on how to achieve the next states that complement the generic guidance provided by the kernel.

In Part III of the book we showed the same team applying a number of other practices to run the entire development from idea to production. Examples of these practices include establishing a stable architecture (skinny system) and achieving acceptance. There are many practices a team could apply across the life cycle of a development endeavor, from pre-development to development to post-development (see Figure 18-4). For example, the team might use the product planning practice to agree on product ideas worth developing and commercializing. The team might use the architecture tradeoff analysis practice to agree on a candidate architecture, and the architecture-centric development practice to confirm the architecture early in the software

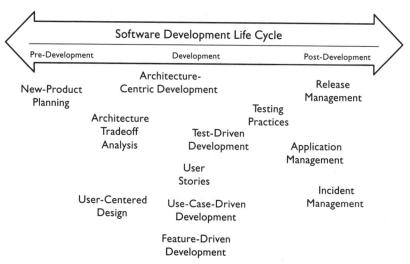

Figure 18-4 Practices across the software life cycle

system's life cycle. If the user interface for the software system is complex, the team may choose to use the user-centered-design practice.

During development the team might use user stories, use-case-driven development, feature-driven development, or test-driven development. Finally, during post-development, the team might use practices for release management. During the software system's operation the team might use some application management practices to ensure that the software system runs smoothly, and incident management practices to handle software system faults, alarms, and warnings.

Each practice listed in Figure 18-4 provides additional guidance to the development team for different stages of the software development life cycle. The practices may introduce additional alphas (see Figure 18-5), such as the following.

- A backlog-driven development practice may add the Requirement Item alpha.
- An architecture practice may add an Architecture alpha.
- An iterative development practice such as Scrum may add an Iteration or a Sprint alpha.
- A component-based development practice may add a Component alpha.
- Test practices may add a Test alpha.

But all of these are outside the kernel—they are added by practices. They are not essential elements of software engineering and it is up to each team to decide how many of these additional practices they need.

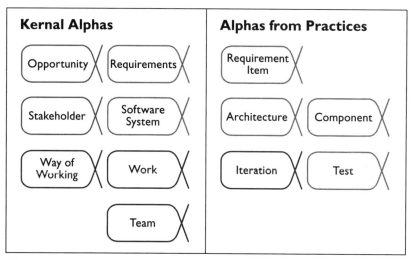

Figure 18-5 Alphas across the entire engineering life cycle

18.4 METHODS IN LARGE ORGANIZATIONS

Large development organizations often engage in many different development endeavors of different kinds. For example, a bank might have development endeavors for enhancing the core banking systems to integrate with other financial institutions or to develop mobile applications to access its services. These different kinds of endeavors have different risks and challenges, and thus might need different compositions of practices and life cycles.

Therefore, an organization can have a prebuilt method for each kind of development endeavor. Each prebuilt method comprises the kernel and a set of practices that are always used. Each team would then use the prebuilt method as a start, and add or remove or modify practices as necessary.

At the same time, large organizations usually have initiatives to improve in certain areas. For example, a large organization might have an initiative to improve software reuse across development endeavors, or to introduce acceptance-test-driven development.

As an example, Figure 18-6 shows a method architecture with three prebuilt methods in a large development organization. Each prebuilt method comprises a set of practices all designed on top of the kernel.

This organization categorizes practices as follows.

- A set of practices that are used in all endeavors. This organization has standardized its defect/issue tracking and configuration management practices.

- A set of practices specific for each type of endeavor. For example, the organization's enterprise integration endeavors apply a modern life cycle (as discussed in Figure 18-2), an emerging architecture, and use cases.

- A set of focus practices to drive its improvement efforts. For example, the organization wants to bring business and IT closer together through acceptance-test-driven development.

Note that each reference method is a starting point for teams to evolve their method—their way of conducting development. The teams are free to add practices as needed, remove practices if they are not mandatory, or modify existing practices.

The method architecture we just discussed is not a vague description of what the organization wants to achieve. Thanks to having precise practices and an extensible kernel, such a method architecture becomes clear and practical.

18.5 PUTTING TEAMS IN CONTROL OF THEIR METHODS

In this chapter we discussed how team members can jointly agree on the practices they will use and consequently build their method.

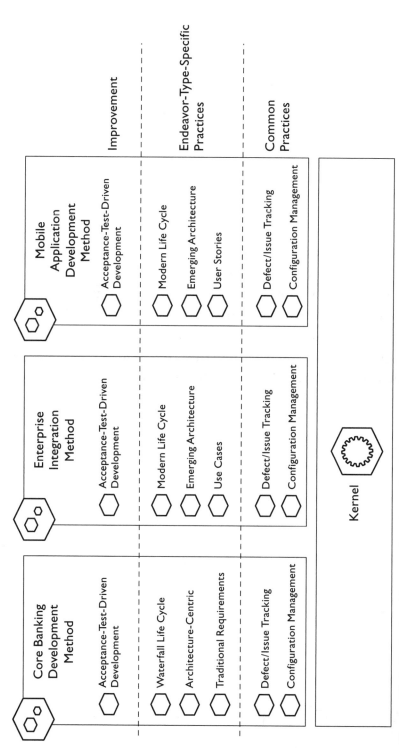

Figure 18-6 Method architecture for a large development organization

In large organizations it is a common phenomenon that the people who dictate a method are usually not the ones who use the method, and worse still, they are usually divorced from the daily challenges on the ground. The development team does not have any influence on their method. This is not good.

While creating new practices (such as user stories, use cases, etc.) is not something a typical development team will do, describing, adapting, and composing in-house practices together is something a team, thanks to the kernel approach, is able to do. This allows the team members to control their own method, rather than have one forced on them.

We also see many development teams attempting to describe what they do so that they can share and discuss how they conduct development. The problem teams face today is that they lack an agreed-on and systematic way to do this. The kernel approach with its precise view of practices fills this gap.

19

Scaling Up to Large and Complex Development

The third dimension of scaling is scaling up from development involving a small number of people to development involving a large number of people. In such cases there is often not one set of requirements, but many; not one software system, but many; not one set of work, but many; not one person in a team, but many; not one single team, but many. In such cases, teams can no longer work in isolation, but must work in collaboration with others. In this situation collaboration and coordination can be very challenging.

Running large and complex development is definitely not easy and involves scope management, prioritization, effort estimation, budgeting, release planning, quality assurance, and much more, which all can be supported by different practices described on top of the kernel. Describing and discussing these practices is outside the scope of this book. What we want to demonstrate in this chapter is how the vanilla kernel can help in large development efforts.

- *A way to design teams:* For large development, it is important to split the work across multiple teams. How should the teams be designed? What are their focuses? How do we ensure that they are collaborating?

- *A way to visualize overall progress:* The different teams are doing their work in parallel. How do we evaluate their progress? How do we provide help to the teams?

- *A way to coordinate development:* The realization of a particular requirement item may demand the participation of multiple teams. How do the teams coordinate their work?

19.1 AN EXAMPLE OF LARGE DEVELOPMENT

Throughout Parts II and III, we showed how Smith and his team worked together as a small team developing a small mobile application. We will now expand this small mobile application story to discuss the value of the kernel for running a large development. When reading this story do not take it as a prescription of what you should do; rather, focus on how the kernel can help you visualize your progress and coordinate your work.

This story involves many requirements, and they are categorized into the following requirement areas (see Figure 19-1):

- Social application requirements, such as networking

- Entertainment application requirements, such as games and music players

- General application requirements, such as customization of a device's home screen, hardware interface requirements, and so on

In a large endeavor such as this, important areas include how you organize the work, how you structure and coordinate the

Social Application Requirements	Entertainment Application Requirements	General Requirements

Figure 19-1 Requirement areas

teams, and how you develop the architecture. The team organization in this story is as follows.

- The customer value team comes up with product requirements through market feedback and watching technology and social trends.

- There are several development teams, one responsible for development and acceptance of each respective requirement area (i.e., the social application requirements, entertainment application requirements, and general requirements).

- Even though each development team tests its own work, there is another acceptance testing team that performs final and independent verification.

In addition to these teams, there are forums to ensure quality architecture, good practices, and good communication among the teams. Forums have representatives from the various teams. For example, there is an architecture forum that is used to achieve consensus on major technical decisions.

There is also a coordination forum that does the following:

- Ensures progress
- Synchronizes work conducted by teams working in parallel

> ### Collaborative Forums Rather Than Top-Down Hierarchies
>
> There are two kinds of approaches to scaling. Traditional approaches tend to be top-down with some group of people "leading" and another group of people "doing." Often the "doing" group has very little voice in how they work and the work is poorly coordinated.
>
> Modern approaches are more participative and advocate self-managing ways of working. Our discussion in this chapter uses the word *forum* to highlight the mechanisms put in place where such participation can occur. In our story there is the architecture forum to deal with major technical issues, and the coordination forum to ensure progress and synchronization among the teams.

19.2 ORGANIZING WORK USING THE ALPHAS

As we mentioned earlier, our large development endeavor has a team organization that comprises a customer value team, an architecture forum, several development teams, and an acceptance testing team.

The kernel alpha states provide a simple way to clarify the focus of each team, as shown in Figure 19-2. Each box in the figure represents a team's focus and contains the six states of the Requirements alpha and the six states of the Software System alpha.

A shaded state means the team needs to focus on the alpha when it is in that state or when it is about to get to that state. For example, the customer value team is focused on the first two states of the Requirements alpha (namely Conceived and Bounded); the architecture forum is focused on achieving the second and third states of the Requirements alpha, and the first two states of the Software System alpha.

Because each team is focused on different areas, its backlog will also be filled with different kinds of backlog items (see Figure 19-3).

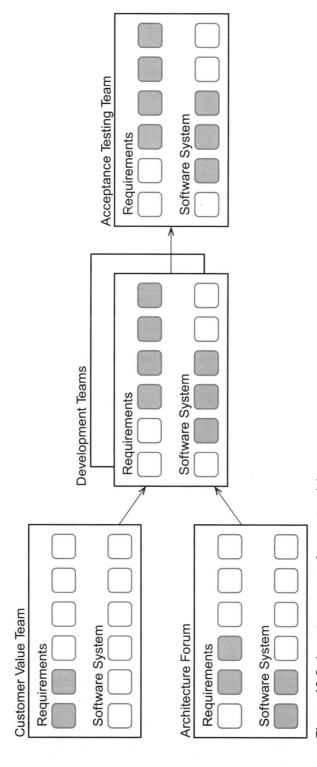

Figure 19-2 Agreeing on team focus using alpha states

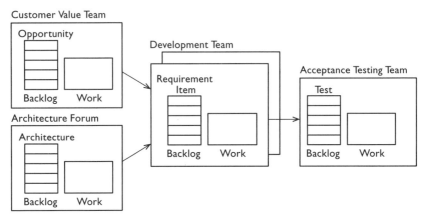

Figure 19-3 Different kinds of backlog items for different kinds of teams and forums

To continue our mobile device story (see Figure 19-3), every team has their own backlog. The development team's backlog is a list of requirement items. Other teams have their own backlogs, but different kinds of items.

- The customer value team is responsible for turning opportunity into reality. They work with a number of opportunity items (i.e., product ideas) to determine their commercial viability. If the opportunity items are viable, the customer value team will use some practices to translate them into a set of requirements to explain them to the development teams. The customer value team will assign a customer representative who will have an end-to-end responsibility for this set of requirements and will work closely with the assigned development team.

- The architecture forum has representatives from the development teams to make architecture decisions, such as which technologies to use, the strategies for allocating run-time resources, how processing should be distributed across computing nodes, and so on. Poor decisions will of course lead to poor architecture. So, early during development, the architecture forum needs to build a backlog of architecture decisions, rank them according to their impact to the software system and development effort, and solve each (or a couple) of them at a time. Note that the architecture forum is not a separate physical team that does not participate in development at all. Instead, all members of the architecture forum are representatives from the development teams.

- As we already discussed, each development team's backlog comprises a set of requirement items. Each team is responsible for the development and delivery of a set of requirement items. So, in our example, there is one development team for the social network requirements, one development team for entertainment requirements, and so on. Each team works closely with their customer representative to fill and prioritize their requirement item backlog.

- Ideally, the development teams should be responsible for the quality of the software system. However, many organizations have an independent acceptance testing team to conduct final verification. The acceptance testing team's focus is to verify the quality of the software system against a set of test items. A test item is basically a set of test cases—for example, a set of functional tests, a set of performance tests, a set of reliability tests, and so on. These test items form the acceptance testing team's backlog.

Agreeing on team focus using alpha states has several advantages. First, the alpha states provide step-by-step guidance to the team on how to achieve progress and health. Second, one can quickly determine if there are missing areas that need to be addressed. For each alpha state, there must be some team focusing on achieving the state. Other teams might be involved but they do not have it as their primary focus. For example, the development teams are responsible for getting the software system to the Demonstrated state, but the architecture forum is also involved in the work to get there.

The Power of Using Alpha States to Create Visibility of Team Focus

When we have observed large software project failures in the past, the root cause has been, more often than not, traceable to a lack of clear ownership within the organization. Aligning team focus with the alpha states ensures that someone is looking out for all the essentials.

19.3 VISUALIZING DEVELOPMENT WITH THE ALPHAS

Agreeing on the focus of each team does not necessarily mean the teams will collaborate well. If each team makes its own plans and runs its own work independently, collaboration across teams will not be effective. Teams need to make their plans and their status visible and easily understandable to other teams, and have mechanisms to discuss progress and remove blockages.

Thus, our mobile device story has a coordination forum, which is made up of representatives from the other teams (i.e., the customer value team, the architecture forum, the development teams, and the acceptance testing team). Both teams and forums conduct their work through the Plan-Do-Check-Adapt cycle as discussed earlier in the book.

- *Plan:* The coordination forum agrees on the current state of development, and plans the iteration. The results of the iteration plan at this level set the objectives for the more detailed iteration planning done by the individual teams.

- *Do:* The teams perform the tasks in their iteration plan.

- *Check:* Each team checks their progress against the agreed-on objectives. The coordination team ensures that any significant progress risks are being resolved by the appropriate teams, and that they are adjusting their plans, if necessary.

- *Adapt:* The coordination forum comes together to review and improve its way of working related to how teams collaborate. Each individual team continues to conduct its local retrospectives.

In large organizations, it is very easy for teams to start doing their own thing and to lose sight of the overall development priorities, due to poor coordination and leadership. Thus, the following is important.

- The coordination forum must ensure that development priorities become the individual team's priorities.

- The individual teams must understand how their progress contributes to the progress of the overall development.

The coordination forum needs a good way to understand the development progress. Here the kernel alphas (in this case the Requirements alphas) become useful. They provide a way to understand the current state of the software endeavor (see Figure 19-4).

Each row in Figure 19-4 depicts the current state (shaded) of the requirements' alphas on the left and their associated current state of requirement items (as a burndown chart) on the right. Here you can see that work on the requirements for the social application requirements is lagging behind other requirement areas.

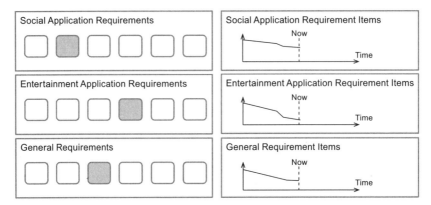

Figure 19-4 Current states of requirements and requirement items

- It is lagging in terms of the team's general understanding of the requirements.

- It is lagging in terms of the percentage of requirement items completed.

This is very similar to the approach we discussed earlier in the book for planning iterations—that is, to determine the current and next states of development, and to determine how to achieve the next states. But whereas what we discussed earlier in the book was for a small development, now we are doing this for a large development.

19.4 COORDINATING THE DEVELOPMENT TEAMS THROUGH ALPHAS

Recall that in Part II we talked about making work visible to team members through task boards and requirement item state tracking. The story in Part II was about a small team. Now we will extend the use of task boards and requirement item state tracking to large development teams. We will focus our discussion on requirement items according to their criticality and impact on the software system as follows:

- Noncritical requirement items

- Critical requirement items

- Crosscutting requirement items

Figure 19-5 shows an example of task boards with requirement items used by the coordination forum and the individual development teams.

- *Noncritical requirement item:* In the simplest case, an individual team can manage without much collaboration with the other teams. This applies to noncritical requirement items (denoted by requirement item "A") that are simple and that the team can deliver by itself. It does not affect other teams. In this case, the team can more or less work on its own.

- *Critical requirement item:* Sometimes a requirement item that an individual development team is responsible for bears great significance to the overall development, which is denoted by "B" in Figure 19-5. For example, the ability to "Browse photos offline" is very important to the success of

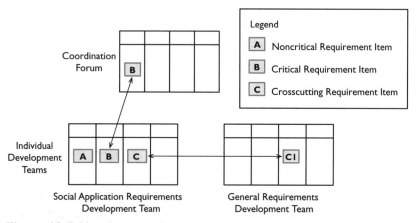

Figure 19-5 Visualizing work across teams using task boards with requirement items in large software endeavors

the overall development. Thus, at the coordination forum it is useful to have this requirement item highlighted. As such, it appears in both task boards.

- *Crosscutting requirement item:* Sometimes requirement items are complex and cannot be allocated to a single requirement area. In this case, they have to be allocated to more than one development team. In most cases, one team is chosen to have primary ownership, and is responsible for collaborating with other teams if necessary. This is exemplified in Figure 19-5 by requirement item "C," which the social application requirements team is responsible for. This requirement item depends on another requirement item, "C1," in the general requirements team. You just need a simple way to label each requirement item such that their relationships can be easily inferred. In our example, we use the prefix "C" to highlight the relationships. In practice, you can choose other techniques, such as using colors or some numbering scheme. Regardless, they help the teams understand their contribution to the overall development.

19.5 EMPOWERING TEAMS TO SCALE

In this chapter we discussed an example of how to run a large development, and the value of the kernel alphas as tools to organize work, visualize progress, and coordinate work among teams.

Traditional approaches to large-scale development tend to be top-down and management-directed, with little regard for the dealings and feelings on the ground. The result can be poor coordination and poor understanding of progress, resulting in unnecessary delays and bottlenecks.

Giving team members a voice in how they conduct development raises motivation and provides a sense of ownership. This ownership supports continual identification of blockages, solutions, and ways to improve.

Modern approaches to large-scale development tend toward a more participative and collaborative style. They advocate self-organization and self-management. Whichever approach you choose, the kernel alphas are an excellent tool for organizing work, visualizing progress, and coordinating work among teams.

FURTHER READING

Poppendieck, M., and T. Poppendieck. 2003. *Lean Software Development: An Agile Toolkit* (Boston: Addison-Wesley).

Leffingwell, D. 2007. *Scaling Software Agility: Best Practices for Large Enterprises* (Boston: Addison-Wesley).

Larman, C., and B. Vodde. 2008. *Scaling Lean & Agile Development: Thinking and Organizational Tools for Large-Scale Scrum* (Boston: Addison-Wesley).

PART V

HOW THE KERNEL CHANGES THE WAY YOU WORK WITH METHODS

Having demonstrated how software teams can apply the kernel in the previous parts of the book, now we take a step back and consider how the kernel changes the way you work with methods. Your situation will no doubt be different from the stories we told in the earlier chapters. Your challenges will be different; your constraints will be different. As such, you and your team will need your own specific method. But you need not start from scratch. Instead, you can start from the kernel, together with practices appropriate for your situation.

The reality today is that developers spend a lot of time thinking and working with methods even though they do not know it. It is also important to realize that to be effective and successful with methods, developers have to be agile when working with methods. It is important to empower your team members with the ability to craft their method and have ownership of their method.

20

Thinking about Methods without Thinking about Methods

As a software professional, you are focused on getting your job done: delivering useful and high-quality software on time and on budget for your customers. But in doing so, you face all kinds of challenges, including the following:

- Getting the real requirements from your customers
- Implementing the requirements correctly
- Choosing the most appropriate technology
- Collaborating with team members
- Ensuring quality in your system
- Ensuring quality in your architecture
- Delivering your system on time

Without a doubt, you have other challenges as well.

20.1 YOU THINK ABOUT METHODS ALL THE TIME

If you ask different software professionals how they handle these challenges, you'll get different answers. Many will say it depends on the specific situation and the characteristics of the development endeavor. Here are some examples.

- Are you developing a brand-new system, enhancing an existing system, or integrating two separate systems?
- Are you exploring the feasibility of some new technology?
- Are you developing a mobile application, a large military system, or a banking system?
- Are you doing in-house development, doing offshore development, or outsourcing the development?

The implication is that when you think about how to deal with your challenges, you think about methods without necessarily being aware of it, *and* a method must adapt to the particular context: the team, the technology, and the environment. Some teams are successful with user stories in a Web development environment, but another team building a military system may find user stories insufficient. To be successful *your method* must help *you* develop great software making *your customers* happy.

Thinking about and discussing different approaches to solve current challenges often takes more time and effort than you you would expect. This impacts different people in different ways. A developer who just graduated from college is often given narrowly scoped responsibilities, which limits the challenges faced and the need to think about methods. On the other hand, experienced software professionals can spend significant time thinking about the way they work. They also have to spend time discussing and agreeing upon it with the other team members, which can lead to long and frustrating debates.

The time spent thinking about methods is longer if your teammates have different backgrounds, experiences, or levels of competence. The time is also longer if the members of your team don't have an effective way to share knowledge.

20.2 DOING RATHER THAN DISCUSSING

Ideally, you should spend very little time talking and discussing software development methods. You should spend more time doing software development. To do this you need to have a good way to think about how you work and to improve it. This is what the kernel does for you. For example, it helps you do the following:

- Reach an agreement with your teammates quickly
- Become more effective in finding the answers to your development challenges

The kernel helps to make methods a natural part of the way you work so that you use and improve your method as you work without even thinking about it.

21

Agile Working with Methods

To be successful you need to be agile, light, and lean in everything you do when working with methods. This doesn't mean you must choose an agile way of working. Rather, it means you must be lean in how you build and adapt your method. When you develop software, you learn new things all the time, and you can improve how you work based on that experience.

The agile movement in the early twenty-first century drew attention to the value of people and teams. It emphasized customer involvement and customer satisfaction and the need to continually evaluate and improve the way the team works.

In contrast to many previous method initiatives, the focus of SEMAT is on those who know best what works and what doesn't work when building software systems—that is, architects, analysts, designers, programmers, testers, and software managers. This takes a change in mindset. It requires a change in the way you think about methods, just as moving to agile development from traditional development requires a change in your mindset. What are the mindset changes you need to be aware of? To some extent they are inspired by those behind the Agile Manifesto.[1]

---

1. http://agilemanifesto.org/principles.html

- The full team owns their method, rather than a select few.

- Focus on method use rather than comprehensive method description.

- Evolve your team's method, rather than keeping your method fixed.

It is worth delving deeper into each of these mindset changes, which is what we will do in the following sections.

21.1 THE FULL TEAM OWNS THEIR METHOD, RATHER THAN A SELECT FEW

Traditionally, there is a dichotomy between method engineers and method users (i.e., developers).

- Method engineers who define methods often do not use the methods themselves.

- Method users who acquire real experiences with methods often are not asked, or do not have time, to give feedback and refine the methods.

As a result, method users find method discussions to be out of touch with their real experiences, and therefore a waste of time.

The kernel approach seeks to bridge this divide by placing a proper balance on all stakeholder perspectives. It recognizes the value of every team member in determining what ways of working work best for the team.

In the preceding chapters, we demonstrated how the kernel can assist in balancing a team's work through the use of alphas, states, and checklists, and by describing a team's own method through a composition of practices. Examples include

- Conducting retrospectives guided by the alphas and their states

- Defining practices on top of alphas and their states

- Using alphas and states to agree on team member involvement and team responsibilities

- Using alphas and states to define life cycles

The alphas and their states and checklists provide a very simple but powerful tool, which team members can employ to take ownership of their own method.

21.2 FOCUS ON METHOD USE RATHER THAN COMPREHENSIVE METHOD DESCRIPTION

Traditionally, when most people talk about methods they are thinking in terms of method descriptions. Having a method description is a good thing in that it allows new team members or even existing team members to familiarize themselves with the team's method. Too often, however, these method descriptions fall short in communicating what team members really do in their day-to-day work. Unfortunately, these method descriptions have often become too heavyweight. This has only served to make the method description less, rather than more, useful.

This dilemma is not best solved by more words, but rather by fewer words and more use. How do teams and team members actually use methods to help them in their day-to-day jobs? Consider the following needs with respect to a team's method.

- Teams need a way to determine real development progress.

- Teams need to plan their projects and their iterations, and they need to discuss and agree on what it means to be done.

- Teams need to organize their team members, and agree on team member involvement and responsibilities.

- Teams need to do their work and adapt their way of working.

- Teams need to scale to endeavors of varying sizes to handle varying challenges and complexity.

These are examples of a team's real needs that the kernel approach can help you address, as we have seen in Parts I through IV of this book.

21.3 EVOLVE YOUR TEAM'S METHOD, RATHER THAN KEEPING YOUR METHOD FIXED

There is no one-size-fits-all approach when it comes to methods. This implies several things.

- You cannot simply take any method and follow it blindly. All methods must be adapted to fit your situation.

- Once the methods are adapted to your current situation, you are certain to learn more as your endeavor proceeds, requiring more adaptations.

A team's method is never fixed. Teams must constantly evolve their method as long as there is work to do on the product. This implies two fundamentals.

1. Always be ready to embrace new and better ways of working.

2. But always consider your current development situation when considering a change.

Evolving a method is simple with the kernel approach. You start with the kernel, and evaluate the practices you already have. Practices that are inadequate are then refined or replaced with better ones. This is best done gradually so that continuous improvement becomes natural and not something you need to think about at great length.

PART VI

WHAT'S REALLY NEW HERE?

This is not the first attempt to find a way to work with methods, so we are not starting from scratch. The software community has been doing this for 50 years or more. However, previous attempts have not been very successful in reaching out to the large number of professionals working with software. This initiative with the kernel and SEMAT in general has carefully studied previous attempts and why they have failed in getting more people interested. We learned what works and what doesn't. We identified several key problems or challenges that we addressed in a fundamentally new way. In this part of the book we will summarize the key differentiators of the SEMAT approach and how they will make a difference to software professionals producing the software we all rely on.

22

Refounding Methods

There are 16 million developers in the world in 2011.[1] Let's say there are 16 developers per team (such teams are big). That would make 1 million teams. Since every team has its own method, there would be 1 million methods. Okay, maybe not 1 million, but at least on the order of hundreds of thousands of methods. Even if we shift our discussion from talking about the entire industry of 16 million developers, to organizations having 1,000 developers or even 30 developers, we do see teams using apparently different methods within a single organization—often as many as ten different methods in an organization with 1,000 developers. The problem is that each method is like an isolated island separated from the other methods by "a sea of confusion" and with no shared common ground. To solve this problem, we need a renaissance in working with methods.

22.1 NOT A LACK OF METHODS, BUT A LACK OF A FOUNDATION—A KERNEL

The problem today is not the lack of methods, or even the lack of good methods. The problem is that the way we work with

---

1. www.prweb.com/releases/2011/9/prweb8834228.htm

methods is not effective—we cannot adopt new ideas into our methods easily; it is difficult to learn from others and build on the success of others. We, as software professionals, need a renaissance for methods.

Fortunately, SEMAT has recognized that there is a common ground underlying all methods. This should not be a surprise. The software community has developed software for more than 50 years. Irrespective of the code being written, the software system being built, the solution being constructed, the methods employed, or the organizations involved, there is a common ground—a kernel of elements that are always prevalent in any software endeavor.

Finding the right elements of the kernel is crucial. They must be universal, significant, and relevant elements guided by the notion that "You have achieved perfection not when there is nothing left to add, but when there is nothing left to take away."[2] SEMAT is also ensuring that these elements are widely agreed on.

In addition to ensuring that the kernel is suitable as a common language for developers, we must also ensure that it helps address developers' challenges and is useful in their everyday lives; that is, it must be practical. In fact, this is the basis for everything we do. On top of this basis, SEMAT seeks to make the kernel both actionable and extensible, as shown in Figure 22-1 and discussed in the following sections

22.2 THE KERNEL VALUES PRACTICALITY

The rationale for the kernel is to make the lives of software professionals easier by making methods more practical and intuitive.

---

2. Antoine de Saint-Exupéry

Figure 22-1 Founding principles behind the kernel

- *Method use over method definition:* In the past many soft-ware initiatives have only paid interest to method definition, namely how to capture methods. They have not focused on how to support the use of a method while actually working in a software endeavor. Thus, the methods became shelf-ware, or not relevant for the developers running software development. Instead, the kernel approach supports the developers so that they themselves can take control of their method and allow the method to evolve as their endeavor progresses.

- *What helps the software professional over what helps the process engineers:* Process engineers should serve the needs of soft-ware professionals, not the other way around. "Software professionals are kings; process engineers are knights serving the kings."

- *Intuitive, concrete graphical syntax over formal semantics:* The language is easy for software professionals to under-stand. While it has formally defined semantics the focus is on syntax to aid the practitioner. In particular it emphasizes the use of things like physical cards to help people apply the kernel in a tangible manner.

22.3 THE KERNEL IS ACTIONABLE AND EXTENSIBLE

The kernel is designed to be actionable and extensible.

- **The kernel is actionable.** While it is true that the kernel attempts to provide a concise list of words commonly found in software engineering, it is not a static dictionary that you read. The kernel is dynamic and actionable. By that we mean you can make the kernel come alive. You can use it in real life to run an endeavor (e.g., a project or iteration). It includes the essential elements always prevalent in every endeavor, such as Requirements, Software System, Team, and Work. These elements have states representing progress and health, so as the endeavor moves forward, these elements progress from state to state.

- **The kernel is extensible.** The kernel includes the essential elements that are universal for all software development endeavors. In addition, the architecture behind the kernel allows you to extend the kernel to support your needs (see Figure 22-2). On top of the essential elements in the kernel, you can add practices or guidelines of many different

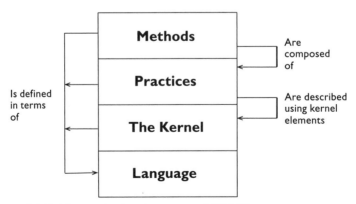

Figure 22-2 The method architecture of SEMAT

kinds, such as support for user stories, use cases, component-based development, architecture, pair programming, daily stand-up meetings, self-organized teams, and so on. You can add these practices on top of the kernel, creating your way of working by composing the practices to build the method you need.

23

Separation of Concerns Applied to Methods

The SEMAT approach to methods is fundamentally different to that used in the past. This can all be summed up with the phrase "separation of concerns." *Separation of concerns* is a principle that you can apply when designing software systems to create systems that are made of nonoverlapping modules, each handling a distinct concern. Separation of concerns helps software systems become extensible and maintainable. Here, we apply the principle of separation of concerns (SoC) to methods, which means

- We specify a kernel
- We make extensions without changing or complicating the kernel

Not changing or complicating the kernel as you add extensions ensures that you, after learning the kernel, can count on the fact that this knowledge is valid even after extensions are made. The kernel approach also applies to separation of concerns in the following ways:

- Separating the kernel from practices
- Separating alphas from work products
- Separating the essence from the details

This is discussed in more detail in the following sections.

23.1 SEPARATING THE KERNEL FROM PRACTICES

This work started from an observation that our industry had been zigzagging around for 40 years. It zigged to one method and then zagged to the next. Often it felt like it was moving from one extreme to another. While there has been evolution, valuable ideas had often been discarded along the way, only to be rediscovered and rebranded at a later date.

So a better approach is needed; one where you do not need to throw out everything that is true and proven when you want to change how you work; one where you can learn and adopt new ideas readily. Thus, we started to apply the principles of SoC to separate different practices from one another, practices that can be understood and adopted separately from others. As we attempted to separate practices, we recognized that there is a common ground between methods, which we call the kernel, and the differences between methods can be described through studying differences between practices. Following the principle of separation of concerns, we employed an approach whereby practices extend the kernel without modifying it. The advantage is twofold.

- *The kernel is stable.* First, the kernel provides a common ground. It gives teams a common language, and a common solid foundation to collaborate and achieve progress in their software initiatives independent of the kind of software endeavor, the complexity of their requirements or software system, and the size of their team.

- *Evolve methods practice by practice.* Second, practices are modular units that help teams overcome challenges in their software endeavors. Each team can choose the practices it needs and replace inadequate practices with more appropriate ones. This provides an evolutionary path for the team to grow their method.

23.2 SEPARATING ALPHAS FROM WORK PRODUCTS

Having recognized that practices can be separated from one another and from the kernel, we next recognized the presence of alphas and how they differed from work products (documents).

Traditional approaches to methods often overemphasized the value of documents and document templates as a measure of progress. Agile proponents are right in emphasizing working software over documentation. However, working software alone is insufficient as a measure of progress. There might be missing requirements; the software system might not be easy to change or test; there might be excessive unplanned work; the team might not be collaborating effectively; and so forth. Thus, a team needs to consider progress from different dimensions: requirements, software system, work, team, and so on. This is where the value of alphas can be found. You measure a team's progress based on the alpha states achieved rather than the amount of documentation produced. A team can produce documentation without achieving progress. Our emphasis is on making progress through alpha states, rather than documentation.

This is why we separate alphas from work products. A simple way to remember the nature of alphas is through the phrase

"Aspiration Led Progress and Health Attribute." Alphas have states that help us evaluate the progress of a software endeavor from a certain perspective. Together, all the alphas can be used to help you provide a comprehensive evaluation of a software endeavor's progress. You can also use them to guide your team to achieve progress. Other uses of alphas include the following.

- You use alphas to determine your team's current state, plan the next state, and track your progress.
- You adapt your way of working through alphas.
- You agree on team member involvement and team responsibilities through alphas and their states.

In summary, the principle of separation of concerns allows us to separate out the detailed representations, such as different documents, from the core concepts captured by the alphas.

23.3 SEPARATING THE ESSENCE FROM THE DETAILS

To make the descriptions of the kernel and practices as practical as possible we describe them in layers. We distinguish between what a team needs when they do their job and detailed information of a descriptive and referential nature.

The layered information structure is also very suitable for learning, regardless of whether the learning is done through on-the-job coaching or more traditional classroom training. The cards at the top level serve as reminders of what you need while working and are used by coaches to drive discussion or give teams specific advice based on the present situation. When team members are very focused on the task at hand, they often do not need detailed explanations and excessive training materials.

The cards contain the essence the team needs to be reminded of. If they want to "learn" more, they can consult more detailed materials, such as guidelines. Even then, guidelines should be no longer than a few pages to let the team find what they need quickly. Then, if they really want additional information, they can consult in-depth materials such as papers and books.

24

The Key Differentiators

To conclude, we will summarize what is really new in the SEMAT approach.

- Innovations with methods
- Practical tools to empower software teams and professionals

24.1 INNOVATIONS WITH METHODS

The SEMAT approach to the kernel and software development methods stems from several key innovations in method engineering.

- Being agile when working with methods is a principle applied throughout SEMAT.[1]
- Separation of concerns[2,3] is a fundamental principle that impacts the complete SEMAT initiative.

---

1. We elaborate on this in Chapter 21.
2. www.SEMAT.org
3. We elaborate on this in Chapter 23.

241

- Finding the essence of software engineering and embodying it in a kernel gives us a foundation to build our knowledge to run software projects better, faster, and with happier customers.

- Defining separate practices on top of the kernel allows you to grow your method in an evolutionary way, one practice at a time, to meet your specific needs.

24.2 PRACTICAL TOOLS FOR SOFTWARE TEAMS AND PROFESSIONALS

Being agile when working with methods is a principle applied throughout SEMAT. This led to a strong emphasis on providing practical tools to help software professionals—something they can make use of in their daily lives.

- Alphas: These are essential to understanding the different dimensions of software development and the universal challenges faced by software development teams.

- Alpha states: These help professionals understand the progress and health of software development.

- Cards (state cards and definition cards): These help to make the kernel tangible.

- Precise practices: These help software teams to zoom in on specific details so that they can deal with specific challenges beyond what the kernel provides.

- The ability to scale *out* and *up:* By this we mean applying the kernel and practices to large organizations (with different kinds of software development endeavors) and large developments (with a large number of requirements and people).

In the end, it is all about empowerment: equipping software teams to own their own method and keep it alive, rather than letting it become shelf-ware. It allows the team to evolve their own method as needed so that working with methods becomes a natural part of the job of developing software.

Part VII

Epilogue

The work on the SEMAT kernel started many years ago, and the upcoming standardization by the OMG means a first major milestone is about to be passed. This does not mean the effort is complete. But the thorough work by the SEMAT community means we will have a kernel that is widely agreed on and that can act as a foundation for the work ahead.

25

This Is Not the End

The grand vision of SEMAT (as defined by the Call for Action in 2009) included a bold statement: "We support a process to refound software engineering . . . that includes a kernel of widely-agreed elements, extensible for specific uses . . . ." *Refound* was intentionally a very strong word, suggesting that we are making a fresh start, exactly what we felt was needed to get software engineering to where it should be as a discipline. The call for action statement has been signed by many leading experts around the world, by several large corporations and academic institutions and thousands of supporters. Given this wide support, the expectations of SEMAT are huge. Have we met them? Let's see where we are.

The grand vision was later interpreted by Ivar Jacobson, Bertrand Meyer, and Richard Soley in a Vision Statement.[1] The very first step was to achieve a wide agreement on the elements of the kernel and a small language to describe methods, practices, and the kernel elements.

With the work done by SEMAT and presented in this book, the very first step of the vision is completed.

It seems clear that we will get a new standard. The real question is whether this new standard will make a difference to the

---

1. refer to the SEMAT vision statement found at www.semat.org.

world. Will we be able to reach the millions of software professionals, who so far have had no or very little interest in working with methods? Why would we succeed this time, when so many previous attempts have just reached a small percentage of the many millions of software professionals around the world? To be successful we need to significantly impact the area of software development education. We must also show to the industry that our approach is effective, getting better software faster and with happier customers. Moreover, we need to bridge the gap between research and industry, and that can only happen if the framework we suggest helps to better communicate ideas in both directions. We are committed to measuring the results of SEMAT over a three-year period.[2] Without reaching a dramatically larger number of people than what we have done so far, we will not be successful.

As we stated: "This is not the end . . . ."

---

2. refer to the SEMAT three-year vision found at www.semat.org.

26

... But Perhaps It Is the End of the Beginning

"Now this is not the end. It is not even the beginning of the end. But it is, perhaps, the end of the beginning."

—Winston Churchill

The work to give concrete value to the community can now begin. A team of people within SEMAT, advised by a larger group of advisors, formulated a three-year vision of SEMAT, a vision up to and including the year 2014. We quote from the three-year vision:[1]

> The SEMAT community through its participants is expected to develop a whole spectrum of products to support its vision. These products are expected to be released separately and at different points in time over the next three years.

---

1. refer to the SEMAT three-year vision found at www.semat.org.

The Kernel and the Language—Through the work of the OMG a set of kernel elements and a language based on the agreed common ground for software engineering will be established. Its publication will promote and enable a new ecosystem for methods and practices based on an open standard. These kernel elements will encapsulate what we all agree is essential and used by practitioners on every project when delivering software. It will include terminology in a way that aids understanding and communication with respect to what we all agree about requirements, teams, software system, stakeholder, work, opportunity, and way of working.

Tools—A variety of tools (including open source)—either as standalone or plug-ins for existing tools—will become available to enable people to author, browse, compose, compare, question, measure and use practices and methods.

The Practice Market Place—The open standard kernel and the language will enable the publication, cataloging, and exchange of practices. The marketplace can in that way help software professionals to quickly establish the way of working that is best suitable in their specific context.

It will be a competition where proven practices as well as new innovative ideas are easily accessible.

Curricula—A new and more systematic foundation for teaching software engineering will emerge, which supports learning in academic and professional environments. Curricula based on the kernel, the language, practices, and methods will be developed and used both in computer science and software engineering programs in our universities.

Textbooks and Papers—New textbooks and reference material to support curricula and personal development based on the kernel and the language will be authored and made publicly available. Many books on practices defined using the kernel that target different level of users will be written to support software professionals in improving their way of working.

Research—The objective nature and ability to tailor, use, adapt, and compare practices will result in a renaissance of software engineering research. Researchers have a common infrastructure, serving as a test-bed and fast deployment of new ideas (extensible practices).

The final objective of all of this is that it will help the industry represented by its practitioners, and the academic world represented by instructors and researchers, in their missions. As we already said, the final outcome must lead to a community where we all build significantly better software faster and with happier customers and users. Moreover, as we also already said, these need to be measurable results, not just ambitions.

27

When the Vision Comes True

Assuming our vision comes true, you may ask yourself, "So what?" What value will this give us as a community? Let's consider the impact SEMAT will have on three key stakeholders:[1]

- The software professional
- The industry
- The academic world

27.1 THE SOFTWARE PROFESSIONAL

When students leave university today and enter the industry, they can directly apply certain skills they have learned (such as Java or C++), but there is a great deal they still must learn. Some of this is unavoidable, such as terminology unique to a given industry, but today even the use of terms as fundamental as *requirements* and *team* can vary widely from one company to the next.

Today change is the norm and people change employers often throughout their careers. When a software professional moves

---

1. This chapter is adapted from SEMAT's Three-Year Vision paper.

from one job to another in a different company, or even in a different part of the same company, she can take her experience with her, but there is a great deal that she must relearn within the new environment. This can discourage the software practitioner to the point of deciding to seek a different career path.

Establishing a standardized kernel is not about excluding anyone; rather, it is about being inclusive and bridging gaps. A set of kernel elements based on industry-wide consensus encourages new approaches appropriate to the job at hand, and ensures that things are not unnecessarily reinvented.

So, what does this mean for the software practitioner? Software practitioners of the future will have more opportunities for employment. They will have greater cross-company mobility and they will be quicker at getting up to speed in new roles.

They will know that what they learn in the university can be counted on when they move into industry, and as they move from one company to another within the industry or from one project to another within a company. Knowing they have learned the essentials will also bring greater self-confidence and self-fulfillment. This is because software developers will be able to focus more of their limited time on the unique aspects of the job that bring value to themselves, their employers, and their customers. They will also know that if they come into a dysfunctional software endeavor they have the ability to articulate to managers exactly how the dysfunctional situation can be evaluated, and made better, faster, and happier. And they can do this using language that the managers already know because the language will have been widely accepted across the software industry.

27.2 THE INDUSTRY

All organizations care about the health of their projects, and they want to know what to do in the face of trouble. Effective checklists can help managers find problems early and know when action is needed. Checklists are integral to the kernel approach.

One-size-fits-all corporate standards cannot provide the answer. Varying factors among teams, projects, products, and organizations must be considered.

To the program manager working in the software industry, the kernel provides a consistent accepted reference of essentials across all her projects, irrespective of size or situation.

To the team leader establishing a way of working suited to his new project, an understanding of the kernel can provide the guidance to select appropriate ways of working to support his team. It also means less ramp-up time when assigning people to projects because they have a common ground and a common vocabulary to build their work on.

To the process professional, the kernel provides a means to communicate how an organization works in a format easily digestible by established employees and new recruits alike—an easily digestible format that improves adoption, facilitates reuse, and provides teams a way to incrementally improve their accepted way of working.

27.3 THE ACADEMIC WORLD

Looking at today's software engineering education, different universities and professors have different ideas of how software engineering should be taught, and what should be taught. Some accreditation guidelines exist. Examples include the Accreditation Board for Engineering and Technology (ABET) in the United States and the SWEBOK *Curriculum Guidelines for Undergraduate Degree Programs in Software Engineering*. However, these tend to provide guidelines at a very high level, leaving (too) much to be defined by individual universities and professors. Variety and freedom is of course a good thing, but the lack of a core set of widely agreed-on kernel elements results in incompatibilities and flavors without any real value-add.

To academia, a widely agreed set of kernel elements can provide a foundation to (1) teach software engineering, (2) design software engineering curricula, and (3) demonstrate to students the pros and cons of different ways of working. A core consensual set of kernel elements ensures that we can understand one another regardless of which university we attended, and will accelerate research and evolution as researchers then can focus on differentiators rather than basics.

From a research perspective, a consensual set of kernel elements provides a reference for the conduct of experiments on different software engineering approaches relevant to real-world problems, and a solid foundation to aid the separation of hype from reality.

27.4 AN EXCITING FUTURE

The original SEMAT call for action, as formulated in September 2009, pinpointed the concerns and issues that challenge the field of software engineering, such as the reliance on fads and fashions, the lack of a theoretical basis, the abundance of unique methods that are hard to compare, the dearth of experimental evaluation and validation, and the gap between academic research and its practical application in industry.

A lot has happened since then. The first step to discover "a kernel of widely agreed-on elements"—the common ground of software engineering—has almost been completed. The kernel as described in this book has been submitted to the OMG and we are waiting for final approval.

Several SEMAT chapters across the world have been established to continue to promote this work. Organizations are now applying the kernel. Universities are now incorporating the kernel into their curricula.

So we feel that the momentum is there and that we will reach our vision. We hope that now you, after reading this book, will be inspired to apply the SEMAT approach in your daily work, regardless of whether you are a student, professor, or software professional. Good luck!

FURTHER READING

Jacobson, I., S. Huang, M. Kajko-Mattsson, P. McMahon, and E. Seymour. "SEMAT: Three-Year Vision." *Programming and Computer Software* 38(1):1–12, DOI: 10.1134/S0361768812010021.

Request for Proposal (RFP): "A Foundation for the Agile Creation and Enactment of Software Engineering Methods" for a kernel and a language.

Humphrey, W.S. "Why Teams Need Operational Processes." Software Engineering Institute, Carnegie Mellon University, November 2009.

Humphrey, W.S. "The software quality challenge." *Journal of Defense Software Engineering,* June 2008.

Boehm, B., and A. Jain. 2005. "An initial theory of value-based software engineering." In Biffl et al. (Eds.), *Value-based Software Engineering* (Springer).

Jones, C. "Scoring and evaluating software methods, practices, and results." Capers Jones & Associates.

Jones, C. "Analyzing the tools of software engineering." Capers Jones & Associates.

Bjørner, D. "The Triptych process model—Process assessment and improvement." From a seminar at Tokyo University in Honor of Kouichi Kishida's 70th Anniversary, 2006.

APPENDIXES

Appendix A
Concepts and Notation

This appendix provides a summary of the key concepts used in the book and their graphical notation.

Table A-1 Terminology and Notation

Concept	Icon	Description
Method		A composition of practices that describes a team's way of working.
Kernel		A set of elements used to form a common ground for describing a software engineering endeavor.
Alpha		An element (an attribute) of a software engineering endeavor, which has a state relevant to assess the progress and health of the endeavor.
		Aspiration Led Progress and Health Attribute is the mnemonic.
Activity space		A placeholder for something to be done in the software engineering endeavor.
Activity		Defines one or more kinds of work items and gives guidance on how to perform these.

continues

Table A-1 Terminology and Notation (*continued*)

Concept	Icon	Description
Work product		An artifact of value and relevance for a software engineering endeavor.
Competency		A characteristic of a stakeholder or team member that reflects the ability to do work.
Practice		A repeatable approach to doing something with a specific purpose in mind (to address a specific challenge).

Appendix B
What Does This Book Cover with Respect to the Kernel?

In this book we introduced a number of concepts from the kernel, and how you can use them in your software endeavor. However, as we did so we inevitably also added our experiences and adaptations. We would also like to say that this book does not describe the entire kernel, but an important part of it, namely: alphas, their states, checklists, and the ability to extend the kernel. So, as a reader you might like to know what parts of the kernel are left out of this book, and what are the things we add on top of the kernel in this book. The intersection between the kernel and this book is illustrated by Figure B-1.

B.I INSIDE THE KERNEL, AND INSIDE THIS BOOK

The book focuses on two specific areas of the kernel.

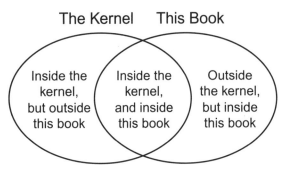

Figure B-1 Scope of this book

- *Kernel usage:* In this book we introduced the kernel alphas (i.e., Opportunity, Stakeholders, Requirements, etc.) and how you use the alphas, their states, and checklists to help you run a software endeavor.

- *Kernel extension:* In this book we also introduced how you extend the kernel by adding practices to yield the method, which you need to help run your endeavor.

B.2 OUTSIDE THE KERNEL, BUT INSIDE THIS BOOK

In this book we demonstrated how the kernel can help you develop good software by telling stories. The stories included descriptions of some of the practices the teams used, practices which are not part of the kernel.

Only the alpha states and their criteria (checklists) are part of the kernel. These are physically represented by the state cards. The techniques and adaptations used in the stories and examples are outside the kernel. Examples of items discussed in this book that are outside the kernel include

- Task boards
- Iterative development

- Life cycles
- Requirement items
- Specific practices
- All dimensions of scaling

B.3 INSIDE THE KERNEL, BUT OUTSIDE THIS BOOK

There are a number of things inside the kernel that we did not discuss in detail in this book. The full scope of the kernel can be described using the method architecture of SEMAT (refer to Figure 22-2).

The kernel language describes the language constructs. We used a number of constructs in this book: alphas and their states, methods, practices, and the kernel itself. The notation (see Appendix A), the well-formed rules governing the use of the notation, and the meaning of the notation are part of the kernel language. Thus, there is a lot more to the kernel language than just the notation. There are also rules governing their practical use.

The kernel comprises a set of elements (which are known as *universals*) defined using the kernel language. The specific kernel alphas, such as Opportunity, Stakeholders, and Work, are part of the kernel.

So, what's in the kernel that we did not discuss in this book? Topics include the following:

- Kernel language
- Areas of concerns
- Activity spaces
- Competencies

Appendix C
Bibliography

C.I SEMAT WORKING DOCUMENTS

[1] Jacobson, I., S. Huang, M. Kajko-Mattsson, P. McMahon, and E. Seymour. "SEMAT: Three-Year Vision." *Programming and Computer Software* 38(1):1–12, DOI: 10.1134/S0361768812010021.

[2] Jacobson, I. "Discover the Essence of Software Engineering." *CSI Communications,* July 2011.

[3] The approved version of the Request for Proposal (RFP): "A Foundation for the Agile Creation and Enactment of Software Engineering Methods" for a kernel and a language. (This supersedes the full draft previously available.)

(Reading tip: Sections 1–5 introduce general rules for OMG proposals and standards; the actual technical content starts in Section 6.)

[4] The highlights of the Request for Proposal (RFP): "A Foundation for the Agile Creation and Enactment of Software Engineering Methods" for a kernel and a language.

[5] A full draft of the Request for Proposal (RFP): "A Foundation for the Agile Creation and Enactment of Software Engineering Methods" for a kernel and a language.

[6] The SEMAT vision statement by Ivar Jacobson, Bertrand Meyer, and Richard Soley.

[7] Jacobson, I., and B. Meyer. "Methods Need Theory." *Dr. Dobb's Journal,* 6 August 2009.

[8] Jacobson, I., and I. Spence. "Why We Need a Theory for Software Engineering." *Dr. Dobb's Journal,* 2 October 2009.

C.2 SEMAT: OTHER DOCUMENTS AND REFERENCES

[9] Funding opportunity from Microsoft with goals relevant to SEMAT: Microsoft SEIF Awards.

[10] Jacobson, I., P.W. Ng, and I. Spence. 2007. "Enough of Processes: Let's Do Practices." *Journal of Object Technology* 6(6):41–67.

[11] Kruchten, P. "A conceptual model of software development." In "Software Project Management with OpenUP," draft, April 2007.

[12] Humphrey, W.S. "Why Teams Need Operational Processes." Software Engineering Institute, Carnegie Mellon University, November 2009.

[13] Humphrey, W.S. "The software quality challenge." *Journal of Defense Software Engineering,* June 2008.

[14] Brown, A.W., and J.A. McDermin. 2007. "The art and science of software architecture." In European Conference on Software Architectures, Lecture Notes in Computer Science, 4758:237-256.

[15] Boehm, B., and A. Jain. 2005. "An initial theory of value-based software engineering." In Biffl et al. (Eds.), *Value-based Software Engineering* (Springer).

[16] The EA-MDE Project: Evaluating Success/Failure Factors of MDE in Industry. Reference person: Jon Whittle.

[17] Bellekens, G. The Modelling Method.

[18] Jones, C. "Errors and omissions in software historical data: Separating fact from fiction." Capers Jones & Associates LLC.

[19] Gilb, T. Undergraduate basics for systems engineering.

[20] Gilb, T. A conceptual glossary for systems engineering.

[21] Jones, C. "Scoring and evaluating software methods, practices, and results." Capers Jones & Associates LLC.

[22] Jones, C. "Analyzing the tools of software engineering." Capers Jones & Associates LLC.

[23] Jones, C. "Software quality in 2010: A survey of the state of the art." Capers Jones & Associates LLC.

[24] Jones, C. "A short history of the cost per defect metric." Capers Jones & Associates LLC.

[25] Cockburn, A. "I Come to Bury Agile, Not to Praise It." Keynote presentation at Agile 2009.

[26] Cockburn, A. "Foundations for Software Engineering." Available online: http://alistair.cockburn.us/Foundations+for+Software+Engineering.

[27] Cockburn, A. "Software engineering in the 21st century" presentation.

[28] Cockburn, A. "From Agile Development to the New Software Engineering." Available online: http://alistair.cockburn.us/From+Agile+Development+to+the+New+-Software+Engineering.

[29] Jones, C. Position paper: "Critical problems in software engineering." Capers Jones & Associates LLC.

[30] Bjørner, D. 2008. "From Domains to Requirements." In *Concurrency, Graphs and Models,* pp. 278–300 (Springer).

[31] Bjørner, D. "The Triptych process model – Process assessment and improvement." From a seminar at Tokyo University in Honor of Kouichi Kishida's 70th Anniversary, 2006.

[32] Jackson, D. "A direct path to dependable software." *Communications of the ACM* 52(4), 2009.

C.3 OTHER REFERENCES

[33] Ng, P.W. and M. Magee. "Light Weight Application Lifecycle Management Using State-Cards." *Agile Journal,* 12 October 2010.

[34] Jacobson, I., I. Spence, and K. Bittner. *Use-Case 2.0* ebook.

[35] Meyer, B. 2009. *Touch of Class: Learning to Program Well Using Object Technology and Design by Contract* (Zürich, Switzerland: Springer-Verlag). Translations: Russian.

[36] Meyer, B. 1997. *Object-Oriented Software Construction, Second Edition* (Reading, MA: Prentice Hall).

About the Authors

Dr. Ivar Jacobson is a father of components and component architecture, use cases, the Unified Modeling Language, and the Rational Unified Process. He has contributed to modern business modeling and aspect-oriented software development. Lately he has been working on how to deal with methods and tools in a super-light and agile way. He has developed a practice concept that is now being adopted by both developers and tool vendors. Now he is one of the leaders of a worldwide network, SEMAT, which is expected to revolutionize software development. He is also the principal author of six influential and best-selling books, and the chairman of Ivar Jacobson International, which has subsidiaries in the United States, the United Kingdom, the Netherlands, China, Singapore, Sweden, and Canada.

Dr. Pan-Wei Ng finds tremendous joy working with developers and software professionals of all levels. He has had great success coaching large-scale systems development organizations, involving many millions of lines of code and hundreds of people per release, through the transition to a lean and agile way of working, not forgetting to improve their code, architecture, and testing through use cases. Dr. Ng is the Asia Pacific CTO and chief scientist at Ivar Jacobson International. He is the coauthor of *Aspect-Oriented Software Development with Use Cases* (Addison-Wesley, 2005). Dr. Ng believes in making things tangible and practical, and has been an active contributor to ideas behind the kernel since its inception. In particular, he invented state cards while helping a large, cross-culture outsourcing development project.

Paul E. McMahon, principal of PEM Systems, has been an independent consultant for the past fifteen years, helping organizations increase agility and process maturity. He has published more than forty articles, many on agile development and lessons using the CMMI. He is a Certified Scrum Master, taught by one of Scrum's cofounders, and a Certified Lean Six Sigma Black Belt. He has more than twenty-five years of engineering and management experience working for companies such as Lockheed Martin and Link Simulation. He has been a leader in the SEMAT initiative since its initial meeting in Zurich. Paul is the author of *Integrating CMMI® and Agile Development: Case Studies and Proven Techniques for Faster Performance Improvement* (Addison-Wesley, 2011), and *Virtual Project Management* (CRC Press, 2000).

Ian Spence is chief scientist and a principal consultant at Ivar Jacobson International, where he specializes in large-scale agile adoptions and practice-based organizational change. An experienced agile coach, he has worked with hundreds of projects to introduce iterative and agile practices, working with development teams ranging from five to one hundred, fifty people. He has also led numerous, successful, large-scale transformation projects in fields as diverse as government, telecommunications, finance, and Internet start-ups, working with development organizations of five to five thousand people. His current interests are agile for large projects, agile outsourcing, and driving sustainable change with agile measurements. He is also the coauthor of two influential software development books, *Use Case Modeling* (Addison-Wesley, 2002) and *Managing Iterative Software Development Projects* (Addison-Wesley, 2007), and was the team lead for the development of the SEMAT kernel.

Svante Lidman is a senior productivity expert at Hansoft AB. Over his twenty-five years in the industry, he has held positions as development manager, program manager, project leader, consultant, and trainer at Ivar Jacobson, Microsoft, Rational Software, and other companies. Svante has for the last five years specialized in large-scale, lean, and agile adoption. Svante is a regular speaker on team dynamics and large-scale lean and agile software development practices.

What People Are Saying about This Book

Scott Ambler

In early 2006, Ivar told me about his ideas around the essentials of the software process and about how to describe them with alphas and work products. At the time, I knew he had some work to do but clearly had important insights to share. This work eventually dovetailed into SEMAT, which I was honored to be involved with at its inception. This book reflects the hard-earned experiences of a host of people, and it is destined to become a classic in the field of software engineering.

—Scott W. Ambler, Founder, AmbySoft Inc.

Dines Bjørner

This book is the result of an intensive effort, SEMAT, originated by Ivar Jacobson. In close collaboration with a string of software engineering consultants, researchers, and practitioners, the authors suggest a basis for software engineering that ties together a number of issues heretofore not adequately covered in the literature. An aim of this book is to provide a basis for both a comprehensive methodology and a theory for software engineering. The book powerfully provides cogent arguments and proposes a number of solutions. I most sincerely hope that this timely book will be studied by many academic researchers and that it will spur widespread discussions and even debates, while at the same time influencing current software engineering and programming methodology research and teaching.

—Dines Bjørner, Ph.D., Dr.h.c., Prof. Emeritus DTU
  Informatics, Denmark

Barry Boehm

There is an increasing need for software process approaches that are sufficiently flexible to fit the variety of development situations that projects will encounter, but that have sufficient integrity to serve as a basis for developing trustable software systems. Having tried to do this by evolving the spiral model and finding how hard it is, I salute the SEMAT developers for converging on a flexible but gently prescriptive approach to cover the full range of software engineering concerns with its kernel of key process, product, and people elements. Its key principles of value-driven system definition and evolution; balancing of near-term agility and architecting for the long term; and attacking risks early and continuously, are critical success factors for coping with software's increasing complexity, dynamism, and enterprise-criticality.

—Barry Boehm, USC, Los Angeles, CA, USA

Capers Jones

This book is not just another surface view of software engineering, but rather an attempt to distill the fundamental concepts of software engineering into an effective model that can be used as a guide for any size and kind of software project. The book considers and addresses all factors that influence software applications, including the need or opportunity that initiates a software project, stakeholders, requirements, and the team who will construct it. The book is not all theory, but includes a number of useful examples based on real problems that many readers will recognize.

—Capers Jones, Vice President and Chief Technology Officer,
  Namcook Analytics LLC

Thomas Atwood

A brilliant approach to bring focus back to the fundamentals in making software projects actually work. I've been most recently involved with websites built using dynamic object programming languages like Ruby, cutting edge app servers like Rails, and a new generation of semantic databases. Agile programming, test-driven development, and powerful application frameworks have made tremendous strides on the technology side. Yet the fundamentals of clearly understanding the objectives of a project, and building development teams that work, has lagged behind. SEMAT's alphas lay it out in a simple, cohesive, and practical fashion. They help everyone who has a stake in the effort, including the customer and the development team, understand the scope and state of the project. Bravo! The distilled wisdom of some of the truly great thinkers who have shaped the software development landscape.

—Thomas Atwood, Ph.D., Director, CloudSuite Media, San Francisco, CA, USA

Arne J. Berre

The SEMAT community should be commended for addressing the identification of a common ground for a much-needed, practice-oriented and adaptive framework for software engineering. It is encouraging to see that the SEMAT Language and kernel also has been contributed as input to a new standard development by the Object Management Group (OMG). This book is an excellent introduction for both practitioners and academics to the principles of this emerging standard and its approach of working with software engineering methods in an agile and lean way.

—Arne J. Berre, Chief Scientist and Associate Professor II, SINTEF and University of Oslo, Norway

Kari Brey

The Essence of Software Engineering: Applying the SEMAT Kernel is what we all have been waiting for. Being a practitioner, and leading organizational transformation in software development for more than ten years, I am often asked why there isn't something written that guides teams on how to be flexible with their approach to delivering software solutions. This book does just that.

The book isn't about a new methodology. It is about the essentials! It is about figuring out which essentials will be needed for each type of effort, whether it be a small team building a small solution or a large distributed team with several interdependencies building large, complex solutions. One size does not fit all and *The Essence of Software Engineering* provides the examples for readers to relate to. The book also stresses the importance of collaborating with the stakeholders, understanding their needs, starting out with building a skinny system and building on that skinny system. I am excited to be a part of SEMAT and even more excited in applying the kernel and sharing those learnings with the software community.

—Kari Brey, Office of the CTO, WellPoint, Inc.

Zhong Chen

Simple is beautiful. You won't be able to imagine how simple and effective the SEMAT way is to address the tough problems of software engineering that have surrounded us for more than forty years, until you read this book–*The Essence of Software Engineering*. The book clearly presents the concise notation, the elegant kernel elements, and the great thought behind the grand vision of "refounding software engineering based on a solid theory, proven principles and best practices." It is a good start to establishing a common ground for practitioners and scholars in the software engineering community, as well as a solid foundation for software engineering education.

The SEMAT initiative, like a fresh breeze, is blowing from west to east, and from north to south over the continents. We can see the new era of software engineering is coming.

—Dr. Zhong Chen, Chairman of SEMAT Chapter in China; Professor and Chairman, Department of Computer Science and Technology, School of EECS, Peking University, China; Deputy-Chair of Software Engineering Teaching Guidance Committee, Ministry of Education, China

Leo Crawford

For too long, software engineers have been embroiled in ideological battles. Initially these were on the placement of braces and the method of indentation. Those battles are mostly behind us, but there are new ones on how we run our software projects—the process and practices we use. I'm delighted to finally see a text that gives us a framework for discussing and comparing the approaches we use—hopefully moving us from religion to science.

—Leo Crawford, FBCS CEng CITP, Cirencester, UK

Barry Dwolatzky

Teaching software engineering within a university curriculum has always been a difficult task. In most other engineering disciplines, one begins by developing a deep understanding of the theory—the foundational principles that hold true over long periods of time. Only once the student has mastered the theory does one introduce specific methods, practices, and applications. The challenge in software engineering is to separate out the foundational principles—the "theory"—from the practice. In *The Essence of Software Engineering*, Ivar Jacobson and his coauthors have tackled the ambitious task of distilling out those essential elements, the "kernel," that lie at the heart of all software engineering methods and practices. This work holds out the promise of giving those of us engaged in teaching software engineering a "theory" upon which to build a coherent and successful curriculum.

—Barry Dwolatzky, Chairman of SEMAT Chapter in South Africa; Professor of Software Engineering and Director, Joburg Centre for Software Engineering (JCSE), Johannesburg, South Africa

Michael Goedicke
The SEMAT initiative provides a range of important possibilities in terms of teaching software engineering. This is a strong motivation for me to engage myself in this activity. The kernel, with its essential notions of software engineering, will enable a systematic and structured teaching. The potential to compare and to assess practices and entire methods will not only be instrumental in teaching and training activities. It also has the potential to identify and categorize new research questions in software engineering!

—Prof. Dr. Michael Goedicke, Specification of Software Systems, Paluno, The Ruhr Institute for Software Technology, University of Duisburg-Essen, Germany; Associate Dean, College of Engineering, Carnegie Mellon University

Martin Griss
This book presents an exciting new way of looking at software development and software engineering. What motivates me as a teacher, researcher, and practitioner of software engineering and software reuse is that for the first time we have a robust basis for a solid product-line approach to describing, analyzing, and running software development processes.

- SEMAT provides a kernel and well-founded building blocks, the essential elements of software development. These elements can be composed, adapted, and extended to describe a variety of well-known methods, such as Scrum, XP, and RUP, as well as newer methods, such as for software services, embedded systems, and systematic reuse. The reusable kernel elements can be enhanced with specific practices to describe details of the method you need.

- Not only can you define and describe your method with precision, but you can also use the selected elements to plan and manage your project. Each element defines specific states that can be used to track progress as the method proceeds through its lifecycle, iterations, or sprints. The state of each element tells you exactly where you are in the project and provides an indication of when you will be done. In particular, laying out the color-coded "state cards" on a table or board can give you an effective dashboard.

- The SEMAT approach can revolutionize the way we teach software development in the future. Students will learn the kernel and how to analyze, measure, and extend different methods. Then students will have a framework to quickly compare the completeness and effectiveness of different methods. They will know how to select and customize a method for a particular situation, and be prepared to perform effectively in a variety of industrial situations.

Jacobson's previous books have led to industry-transforming contributions such as the Unified Modeling Language (UL) and the Unified Process, and so I expect this book too will have an equally profound impact.

—Martin Griss, Ph.D., Director, Silicon Valley Campus

Shihong Huang

As a software engineering professor, I often feel puzzled by how to recognize and convey the core concepts of software engineering, which I can give my students so they are equipped to cope with an ever-changing industry. This book provides a systematic and easy to understand description of the essence of software engineering. The examples in the book are intuitive, the text is easy to follow, and the topics are relevant to industry. We are in dire need of such a textbook in academia. This book is not only a good choice for software engineering courses, but also for general practitioners who wish to excel in their careers. This book will stand as one of the ever-lasting classic software engineering textbooks on the bookshelf.

—Shihong Huang, Florida Atlantic University

Pontus Johnson

The goal of this book is very important: to describe a sound, common foundation for software development. Reaching beyond the hypes, the kernel represents the most important elements of any software engineering endeavor and their relation to each other. From a practical perspective, this allows developers to break free of methodological dogmas and tailor their methods according to their own needs. From a theoretical perspective, the kernel is a frame for a comprehensive theory of software engineering. Such a theory is a Holy Grail of software engineering, elevating the discipline from the travails of trial and error to the province of premeditated design.

—Professor Pontus Johnson, Ph.D., Industrial Information and Control Systems, KTH–Royal Institute of Technology, Stockholm, Sweden

Chao Liu

What is the essence of software engineering? Why should we bother with fundamentals while we study new approaches for solving the problems of software engineering? For a long time, we have not only been faced with a variety of tough problems, but have also been bogged down by the continuously growing number of methods, techniques, and approaches in the field. This book introduces a kernel as a base to understanding software engineering, as well as managing it effectively. It is a unique and very valuable book for anyone with an interest in software engineering. Actually, I have introduced the SEMAT approach in my software engineering courses and also to engineers and managers from the industry where the interest for SEMAT is high.

—Chao Liu, Professor, School of Computer Science and Engineering; Director of Software Engineering Institute, Beihang University, Beijing, China

Barry Myburgh

This book describes a practical and adaptable approach for software engineering. It succeeds where previous attempts at defining adaptable approaches have failed. Instead of starting with a heavyweight process framework and tailoring it for lightweight use, it starts with a common kernel on top of which essential practices can be added to meet the demands of the software engineering situation at hand. We have known for decades that management of software engineering is one of the most difficult things to do, and I am convinced that the SEMAT approach described in this book will be of great help to anyone involved in the management of software engineering!

—Barry Myburgh, M.D. and Principal Consultant, Insyte Information Systems Engineering, Johannesburg, South Africa

Meilir Page-Jones

The SEMAT initiative is a welcome effort to skim away the methodological froth that has long bedeviled us and to reveal the true common core under all software approaches—new and old, fashionable and unfashionable. In this way, managers, practitioners, and academics will be able to compare like with like and therefore make more reasoned discrimination among the smorgasbord of practices and methodologies on offer. I welcome this book, among several other endeavors that seek to promote the SEMAT approach.

—Meilir Page-Jones, Senior Consulting Methodologist,
   Wayland Systems Inc., Renton, WA, USA

June Sung Park

SEMAT, I believe, will make a landmark contribution to the history of software engineering, which was started back in the 1960s. Its main contribution is to generalize and simplify the core principles of human endeavors that lead to high-quality software in a predictable and controlled manner. The kernel and the language are what the software engineering community needed to have as a common base. This common base will allow countless extensions to address specific contexts and goals of software development and software project management, while making those extensions possible to compare and combine to create better and better combinations.

—Dr. June Sung Park, Professor, Industrial and Systems
   Engineering, KAIST; Joint Professor, Computer Science,
   KAIST; Adjunct Professor, School of Management,
   University of Texas at Dallas

Ed Seymour

Fujitsu became involved with the SEMAT initiative because we recognised how the SEMAT vision aligned with our own strategy for reusable software methods and can help us provide consistent, verifiable points of reference without impeding innovation. This book introduces the SEMAT kernel, which promises to deliver consistency, improved reuse, and a scalable approach to suit all delivery models. I believe it can potentially also help businesses improve their governance, in particular when working with third parties and partners, and even their recruitment processes. This book represents a significant milestone in the progression of software engineering.

—Ed Seymour, Principal Solution Architect, UK & Ireland, Fujitsu

Anders Sjögren

Do you see "the light at the end of the tunnel" or "the forest for all the trees"? After reading this book, and discussing the distillation of software engineering the SEMAT initiative provides with my students, I do see "the forest." It feels like the SEMAT approach cleans up and lets us organize what has grown in the field of software engineering over many decades. I also hope that the SEMAT approach will prove valuable, not only to pure "software" endeavors, but also more broadly to ICT engineering projects since we rapidly are moving into "software everywhere" and "Internet of things" where hardware plays an equal role as software. This book is worth reading and adopting for a wide range of students and engineers. A bright star, like SEMAT, may illuminate a lot in a tunnel.

—Anders Sjögren, School of ICT, Royal Institute of Technology (KTH), Stockholm, Sweden; President, Korea Software Technology Training Institution, Korea Software Technology Association

Carlos Mario Zapata

For many years, software engineers have been empirically searching for the "essence" of their discipline. Scholars are also searching for this "Holy Grail" of software engineering. I strongly support the ideas behind SEMAT and especially the idea of a "kernel" as envisioned by SEMAT. This book does not mean that the search is over, but I think it presents the best possible candidate we have for evolving towards our Holy Grail.

—Carlos Mario Zapata J., Ph.D., Chairman of SEMAT
    Chapter in Latin America; School of Systems, National
    University of Colombia

Index